#What's Next After High School

Juliet Murphy

#WHAT'S NEXT AFTER HIGH SCHOOL?

Choosing a Great Career You'll Love:
A Guide for Parents and Students
Working Together

JULIET MURPHY
www.julietmurphy.com

" *Your work is going to fill a large part of your life,*

and the only way to be truly satisfied is to
do what you believe is great work.

And the only way to do great work is to love what you do.

If you haven't found it yet, keep looking.

Don't settle.

As with all matters of the heart,

you'll know when you find it. **"**

—Steve Jobs

Website: www.julietmurphy.com

Email: info@julietmurphy.com

Phone:

Ordering Information: Quantity sales. Special discounts are available on multiple purchases by corporations, associations, and others.

For details, contact the "Special Sales Department" at the address above.

#What's Next After High School , Juliet Murphy --1st edition, 2017

www.evolveglobalpublishing.com

Book Layout: © 2017 Evolve Global Publishing

ISBN: 978-0-9993563-2-6 (Paperback)

ISBN: 978-0-9993563-3-3 (Hardcover)

ISBN-13: 978-0-9993563-1-9 (Createspace)

ISBN-10: (Createspace)

ISBN: 978-0-9993563-0-2 (Smashwords)

ASIN: B071KB3MQM (Amazon Kindle)

This book is available on Barnes & Noble, Kobo, Apple iBooks (digital)

Dedication

My wonderful husband and cheerleader, Brian, who supports me more than I ever could have hoped.

My mom, Jelion. Your strength is my inspiration.

My niece, Simone, who just graduated from high school and who served as my high school consultant in gathering content.

Table of Contents

Introduction

My name is Juliet Murphy. I help parents and their high school students to work together to conduct effective and goal-focused career planning, so they can have careers they love and live the lives they desire.

I am writing this book as a career coach and also as a parent of two young adults who recently completed college.

This book is intended for both parents and high school students. By reading this book, they'll discover that having a rewarding and fulfilling career requires planning and research, and its foundation must be based on something the student truly wants to do. **This is non-negotiable.**

Failing to do adequate planning and research can have devastating results: It can lead to millions of unhappy young adults and parents, with many headaches, much frustration, and multiple start-overs—and sometimes the loss of career traction altogether.

Why I Wrote This Book

Every year, I see hundreds of individuals who are unhappy in their careers, including many young adults who have finished college. They feel confused and are unable to identify what career to pursue or how to translate what they studied in college into a career. Time and time again, I discovered the problem stemmed from their lack of understanding of the career selection process early on. My career is based on helping people. I had to do something to help.

Seeing this mistake repeated over and over prompted me to begin at the root of the problem, which is high school students making uninformed career decisions. Reaching high school students and helping them understand what it takes to truly plan a career is one of the primary solutions to this issue. Even though they're young, they need to think about what their life after high school will be like.

The sooner we take steps to educate people about what it takes to really plan and develop a career, the better it will be because then we'll have more productive, happy people—people who love the work they do and the life they live.

My Qualifications For Writing This Book

I have an extensive background working with new college graduates and the millennial generation; I also have experience working with individuals who were once new high school graduates who didn't make the right career decision. I see them in my office every day, and I help them start over, using their interests and passions to plan and build a rewarding career.

As a matter of fact, I was one of those people who didn't make the right career decision earlier on. I didn't find fulfillment in my work until late in my career. Doing what I do as a career coach is my calling. I love it, and I want everyone else to experience the joy of loving what they do.

Before I started my private practice, I led an award-winning leadership development program for new college graduates for a Fortune 500 company. Currently, I also co-chair an Undergraduate Advisory Board for the business school at the University of Southern California (USC) where I help the school's educators plan curriculum and develop strategies to best prepare graduates for fulfilling careers in the workplace.

I earned an MBA from the University of Southern California and a master's in career development from John F. Kennedy University, but my strongest qualification is the passion I have for helping others. More than anything, I care about young adults. Since I know they're our future, I'm disheartened when I see students who have graduated from college come to me still not knowing what career to pursue. I've seen students who have studied medicine, law, criminal justice, economics, psychology—you name it—and they're not happy in their careers.

This book is designed to stop that situation and help young adults start out right so they can have a happy, fulfilling career doing what they love and making a difference.

Who This Book Is For

The book is for parents and their sons and daughters in high school and middle school, as well as anyone who cares about one of these students or their parents. You'll be doing a tremendous service if you share this book as a resource to help them start their career on the right track.

Why This Book Is So Important

The information and insights I've provided in this book can save students from starting their careers on the wrong foot based on incomplete or wrong information. It's much easier to begin this journey on the right path than to change course midway. As a career coach, I've seen it both ways. The career trajectory of an individual starting off doing something that feels right and natural for them and something they're excited about is so much more rewarding and productive than that of someone who is unsure why they're doing what they're doing and who feels a void in their work.

Functioning, surviving, and trying to prosper in a career that feels unsuitable takes tremendous effort, and often you never rise to your full potential. You end up working twice as hard and never obtain the satisfaction and joy you hoped you would.

Getting an informed start eliminates the need for a career coach late in the game and provides you with the required tools to create a career path and life that you will love. If this book does its job for enough people, I may have to look for a new line of work! But there would be nothing more satisfying to me as a professional knowing that I have changed people's lives by giving them the tools and skills to create the career of a lifetime.

Message to Parents

I want to start by thanking parents for everything you have done to help and support your children to get them this far. The love you have for them can't be matched, and your desire to see them succeed can't be put into words. You're 50 percent of the reason why I wrote this book and your precious son or daughter is the other 50 percent.

As you prepare for your child's "what's next," it's helpful to remember that yes, this is a very important step in life, but very few things are life and death situations, and decisions and indecisions on career choices, is not one of them. However, this is a situation that's critically important and needs to be approached with a healthy dose of trust, faith, and calm so the great things you want and envision for your child can actually come to fruition.

So let's remove the tension and maintain a mindset that success comes in many forms, and even when a particular success path has been trusted and proven, it still may not be the path to success for your child.

What you and your child can both rely on, however, is the love and support you have for each other as you both work through their "what's next."

Message to
High School Students

Graduating from high school is a time of fun sprinkled with tremendous pressure. With high school ending, you're moving into adulthood and have many decisions you need to make quickly, with minimal life experience to do so.

In addition to this, it seems everybody else knows what's best for you, and they're all giving you advice for what you should do next, whether you welcome it or not. You may also be struggling with the changes and responsibilities that are in store as a high school graduate. It can be overwhelming and sometimes even downright scary.

When you're feeling confused or anxious, don't hesitate to tell your parents. Your parents' love and their role in your life are never over. However, as you move into adulthood, it becomes increasingly your responsibility to make your own informed decisions and be active in the decision-making process.

By no means does this mean that you should exclude your parents. In fact, including your parents in your decision-making will be a win-win for both you and them. You both want the same thing, so the clearer you both are on what that is, the better it is for you.

Later in the book, I'll share some techniques and strategies with both you and your parents on how to be candid and open in discussing your thoughts and feelings about your career, your future after high school, and just about anything else on your mind.

Remember that your parents want the best for you—often more than you do for yourself, even if sometimes you think otherwise. This is natural, particularly as you face your last year in high school and it becomes crunch time to make decisions. If, and when, you get these thoughts, just remember that this isn't the time to shut down or be disrespectful. Instead, it's a time to open up and talk.

Never be afraid to let your parents know what you're thinking.

Chapter 1

Which High School Student Are You?

High school is a major turning point in a teenager's life—the time when you begin to feel you're becoming a grownup and independent. The next big decision you'll need to consider is what you'll be doing after high school. Because you're all different with your own sources of motivation and inspiration, you'll each have different thoughts about what's best and what's next after graduation. Below, I've captured some of the most common high school student profiles. Do you see yourself in one of them?

I've Always Known What I Wanted To Do When I Grow Up, And I'm Going To College

Some students have known what they want to do from as far back as they can remember, and that choice never wavers. They may have wanted to be a doctor, nurse, graphic artist, musician, teacher, or other professional, or become a member of the military.

Most of these students stay on track. They have everything all laid out from the get-go. They're ready, they've done their research, they've shadowed someone in their desired field, and they may even have interned or volunteered in the field.

It's something they've always wanted to do because they're passionate about it.

For most of these students, career decision-making isn't much of a challenge. They're on track and they've got this.

I'm Going To College But I'm Not Sure What I'll Be Studying And Why — I'll Figure That Out Later

You're the student who knows you're going to college and will figure out specifically what you want to major in or do when you get there. You want to go to college for a variety of reasons—you know it's a "solid" choice, you want to join a fraternity/sorority, or you'd like to study abroad. Or maybe it's because all of your friends are going to college or because it's simply expected of you.

Whatever the reason, you know with certainty you're going to go to college and you'll figure out the career part later.

I'm The First In My Family To Go To College

You're the first in your family to go to college, and you're going to make your family proud. You're determined and nothing is going to stop you!

There's a lot hinging on your success, and you can't afford to fail as you see college as your only way to success and to make a better life for you and your family. You're extremely committed to getting a higher education, and although you don't have financial or other resources to fall back on, you're resourceful and have the drive and commitment to make it happen. In Chapter 10 you will read Daniela's story.

My Parents Have A Family Business And Want Me To Join It, But I Don't Want To

Your parents have a family business, and they expect to pass the baton on to you so you can continue the family legacy. But there's a problem— you want your own career, and it's not in the family business.

This can be a sensitive challenge and sometimes a heavy weight for a high school student to bear. This is especially so today as the world of work is evolving quickly, and many family businesses may be considered old school businesses that are declining in demand.

Even if your family business is booming, you don't want to take it over, despite your parents' expectations.

You're struggling with how to let them know that you don't want to carry on with the family legacy, while you're still figuring out what you truly want to do for a career. How can you disappoint them?

I Want To Start My Own Online Business After High School

You're the student who becomes easily bored, and high school barely holds your attention. You have many ideas of what you'd rather be doing. You're an independent thinker and believe you can start a successful online business without ever having to leave your room.

You want to do something that interests you. You want to do it now, and college isn't on your radar, but it is on your parents'.

What should you do?

Tip: Don't start skipping school. The first thing you should do is to discuss this with your parents .

I Want To Go To Trade School

A trade school is also known as a technical or a vocational school. You've always been interested in the technical side of things and you're hands on. Or, in some cases, you want to follow in the trade footsteps of mom and dad. You enjoy working on machinery or doing culinary arts, and you want to go to a trade school rather than a traditional four-year college. You've already taken hands-on classes in high school and enjoyed them and would like to pursue them further. You'd like to earn a certificate showing your qualifications and start a job immediately following trade school graduation.

I Want To Start Working Right After High School

You believe that college isn't the only path to career success, and you'd like to start working to earn your own money immediately following high school. A lot of jobs don't require a college degree–you know people who don't have a degree and are doing just fine.

However, with so many people telling you that college is the only guaranteed way to success, you wonder if this is the right choice.

I'm Considering The Military

You've always had an interest in the U. S. military, and you're seriously considering enlisting after high school. You've heard great things about the education and training benefits for enlistees.

You're not sure which branch yet, although perhaps the beautiful overseas bases of the Navy appeal to you or you've always wanted to fly jets in the Air Force. Before you decide, you want to learn more about each branch, the time commitments, benefits, and how all these fit with your future life goals.

I Want To Take A Gap Year Before Thinking About College

The gap year is becoming more common as a year-long break between high school and higher education. This is your last hurrah after high school as well as a chance to step back, pause, and assess your options. You also see it as an opportunity to travel and see the world or to volunteer. You can attend college the following year. Read about Jordan's gap year in Chapter 8.

I'm Still Young – Let Me Enjoy High School – Things Will Fall Into Place

You're young. You only live once so "let me enjoy my high school years and then I'll figure out what to do later." You've done absolutely no planning for what happens after high school. You believe tomorrow will take care of itself. Your parents are concerned, but you're convinced things will work out.

Summary

Although these profiles aren't reflective of all high school students, you'll probably see yourself in one or more of these scenarios. Using our T.R.U.S.T. ™ system in Chapter 7 will help you and your parents talk about all of these possibilities and choices. Whatever your path is, this book will provide a wide range of information that will benefit you as you prepare for the rest of your life.

Chapter 2

Challenges High School Students Face When Choosing a Career

Definition of a Career: an occupation or profession, especially one requiring special training, as one's lifework.

Definition of a Job: a piece of work, especially a specific task done as part of the routine of one's occupation.

Dictionary.com

As you can see from the definitions above, a career involves more training and longevity in the work that you do, whereas a job is a piece of work that can be conducted within a career or otherwise done over a shorter period. You can have many jobs over a lifetime, but typically you'll have only one or two careers.

Throughout life you'll face many challenges, and as a high schooler these challenges will pounce on you before you're prepared to handle them. But, whether you're prepared or not, you'll need to overcome them. One rule of thumb in handling challenges is, if you're not feeling it in your heart, it's okay to make another choice and it's also okay to seek help.

Career Planning Challenges For High School Students

1. Students Don't Have Enough Information To Fully Understand What A Career Is

Many high school students don't know where to begin in contemplating a career. They may have some ideas about different careers, but they really don't have a good handle on them or a good understanding of the "why" and the "how" to get there. The entire career planning and decision-making process can be daunting and overwhelming.

At this stage, students are young and inexperienced and are just starting to think about what they need to do with their lives. Much of their information is coming from their friends and classmates. They're anxious to get out of high school to taste freedom and independence, to go out into the world and make their own decisions and choices. But they really don't know what that entails. They just believe it's going to be awesome.

> **Tip:** *There's a limitless amount of information on the internet. Google any career that you're interested in and there will be information on what it takes to be successful in that field. Two sites you can explore are o*netonline.org and California CareerZone. Even though the latter is a state-sponsored site for California, the information can be accessed by anyone.*

2. The High School Experience Becomes All About Preparing For College

Many high school students are influenced by their environment. As they enter high school, one of the first things they hear is, "Where are you going to go to college?" This becomes the primary question and focus, the goal and guiding principle throughout high school. So the main focus in high school becomes preparing for college.

Because of this, many students believe they have to be focused on college as their number one priority and may miss out on extracurricular activities unless they think those activities will help their college applications.

Focusing too much on getting into college can be a disservice to the student. Why? Because students could miss opportunities to be exposed to other non-college focused classes or opportunities that may push them to consider other areas of interest that could contribute to their career decision-making. They spend too much time thinking about college and not enough time thinking about what they're going to do after college.

That's one of the biggest challenges that high school students face, especially when making decisions is still so difficult for them. One parent told me, "Here's my child; he barely knows how to make his bed and now he's charged with making this big decision of what to do after high school and make all these plans."

It's overwhelming for students, and they need some help in this area.

Tip: *First, take a deep breath and think about some things that you'd like to accomplish during your high school years. This may involve sports, student government, or even something that's not done at your high school—perhaps play an instrument, or do dance or photography. High school is your last time before you have to face the "real world," so it's important you maintain a balance between strong achievements in academics and enjoying your high school years.*

Talk with your high school guidance counselor when their schedule permits and get their input about any class that you'd like to learn more about. Speak with your parents, family, and friends. Set some time aside to, at the very least, read about a class that piques your interest and that you wouldn't typically take.

Consider doing volunteer work in areas that interest you. You won't just learn from your actual volunteer work—you'll meet new people, and you can discuss any questions you have with them about careers and the work they do.

3. Not Knowing How to Choose A College To Attend

Even though there's a great emphasis in high school on attending college, students are still not clear on how to go about choosing the right college. Some students don't spend enough time doing their homework on college selection while others overanalyze.

To help you simplify the process, we've provided some criteria for college selection in Chapter 8 and links to additional information at the end of the book.

Tip: *When in doubt, Google it.*

4. Lack Of Resources For Adequate Career Planning At Public High Schools

Most public schools don't have the staffing for adequate career planning and counseling. When there are 500-plus students waiting for the same school counselor to help them, that leaves little time for each student. As a result, a lot of the decision-making is left up to the students, and most just don't know how to go about this.

Tip: *There are many online sites that you can use to help you figure things out. You can start by Googling "Career Counseling for High School Students" and explore your search results. However, this may be the time to ask your parents to hire a career coach to help you figure things out.*

A qualified career coach can help put you at an advantage by helping you focus on your talents, interests, personality preferences, and values to identify and choose the career that's the best fit for you. Having the help of a professional will save you and your parents' time and money as you'll be making career choices with confidence that you're making the right decision. A coach works with assessments that are validated and proven reliable in guiding career decision-making to ensure that career decisions are in alignment with the teen's aptitude and capabilities. Because assessments create a strong sense of self-awareness, they play an invaluable role in preparing you for college interviews and writing your personal statements as you'll have specific terms and expressions to use when describing yourself. If you'd like to learn more about how a career coach can help you, you may contact us at www.julietmurphy.com .

5. Student And Parents Not On The Same Page

According to a recent study conducted by the Pew Research Center, 58 percent of teens today say their parents are their best friend. This further emphasizes the role of trust and influence parents can have in helping their child with the career decision process.

All parents have high expectations for their child, and a standard expectation is that their child must go to college to secure a better life. But is that really so? Although there are many discussions about which college to attend, there isn't much discussion about whether a child should attend college or not.

For most, it's a given that college becomes a part of the high school student's future. This can cause misalignment between a parent's and student's expectations and goals, and it can become even more challenging if neither feels comfortable debating whether college is a must. Not being able to communicate openly and freely about this can be expensive as the student may head off to college for the wrong reason, or perhaps may select the wrong major.

Teens don't want to disappoint their parents who may be their best friend. So they leave for college without really knowing what they should be doing, how they should be doing it, and what their end goal is.

> **Tip:** *Talk with your parents. Be open and candid and let them know what you're thinking and what major or career appeals to you. Later in the book, we introduce a system to help you have a healthy conversation with your parents.*

6. Failing to Learn From Parents And Others

In today's world, there seems to be minimal time for teens to talk with their parents and other adults to seek advice. With the accessibility of information in the Cloud and the distraction of social media, the opportunity for person-to-person conversations keeps decreasing.

Additionally, high school students have significant amounts of homework, keeping them fully occupied when they get home from school. When you couple that with part-time jobs, extracurricular activities, sports, music, and volunteering, it leaves little time for students to talk with parents and other adults to seek their perspectives.

> **Tip:** *Although this a different challenge from the one above, the same recommendation applies.*

7. Not Knowing It's Okay To Change Plans

Things change. That's a fact of life most adults understand. Life can interfere or circumstances can change, even with the best, most carefully thought-out plans. Knowing that things will change, being comfortable with change, and learning to navigate change will be critical to a student's success in college and in life.

If you go to college, college may not work out, and that's okay. What is not okay is to give up and fail to consider other options. With the right mindset, there are multiple options, whether you stop-out or drop-out.

As a big supporter of education, I understand that becoming educated the traditional way by going to college is important, but I also believe it's not the only way. Many people lead successful lives without ever receiving a college degree. I'm able to write this book on a computer and listen to music on my iPhone because Bill Gates and Steve Jobs dropped out of college at a time when people had no idea the instrumental force they would play in shaping the landscape of modern technology.

I'm not saying you can drop out of college and be the next Bill Gates or Steve Jobs, as the odds of that happening is probably one in a multi-million. I'm merely letting you know that it's all right to change your mind and to alter your life direction. I personally know several people for whom college didn't work out and as soon as they realized it wasn't for them, they changed course. One went into construction; a second (a woman) borrowed money and started a moving business that's growing steadily; and another is working in retail.

One important thing to remember is, even if your teen drops out of college today, it doesn't mean that a college education is lost forever. Sometimes dropping out and pursuing something else is exactly what teens need to realize the value and benefit of college and reposition their focus.

Tip: *You must be honest with yourself first, which in turn will make you honest with others. When things change, go ahead and be brave and say so. Let your parents know. Being afraid is only limiting you and holding you back from your dreams. You still have time to adjust your plans as you do life.*

8. Not Having A Back-Up Plan Discussion

Having a "what if…" plan is an excellent idea as it will help prepare both parents and students in the event their Plan A is unsuccessful. When that happens, they can launch right into Plan B. Having planned for it in advance makes it much easier and less stressful to handle.

Tip: *Be flexible and be willing to explore other options.*

9. Unclear On How Learning In School Applies To The "Real World"

Here's a direct quote from a recent high school graduate who is on her way to college:

"My biggest challenge in high school when it came to deciding what I wanted to do was that I didn't know how what I was learning would apply to the 'real world.' I often found myself learning in order to do well on a test and not necessarily in order to figure out what I'd like to do in the future. Another realization I had was that schools do the absolute minimum to help us decide what we want to do with the rest of our lives."

Tip: *For parents of teens in a similar situation, consider hiring a career coach to help them get an understanding of what they can do as they head off to college to ensure that when they graduate with a two- or four-year degree, they'll be ready for the workplace and for life.*

10. Being Steered in Different Directions As Part Of A Blended Or Divorced Household

Sometimes, the high schooler is faced with not knowing which choices to make because both parents aren't on the same page, such as when there's co-parenting due to divorce or being in a blended household. In situations like these, the student often struggles with balancing all the different suggestions from different sides. This can leave them confused and torn as they don't want to appear to be taking sides. This gets even more complicated if one parent has the financial resources to cover expenses for whatever path the student decides to follow and the other doesn't.

Tip: *The first thing here is to be honest with both parents. Politely acknowledge each parent's suggestions; share with them what you'd like to do for your career; and ask for their support. If you're reading this book and they're not, get them a copy and together use our system to help guide the discussion.*

Chapter 3

Which High School Parent Are You?

As a parent, you've been the center of your child's life and remain a key influencer in what he or she does after graduation.

Until now, you've been directing your high schooler throughout life; you've been in charge. As a result, it's sometimes difficult to let go and allow your student to grow into young adulthood. It's tough. It's a time when they need you and yet they need to be independent.

What do you do? Do you step back and be hands off, or do you continue to parent as usual?

It's important for you as parents to still be available to advise and support your son or daughter but in a different way:

Parents must be willing to adjust the parental role to be more of a consultant to their young adult high school student.

It's important for parents to transition into this role as they support and partner with their young adult. Recognizing this will be a critical tool in working together as a parent/young adult team to help in the career decision-making process. It will also be a signal to your high schooler that you trust and respect them in making responsible decisions that will define their future.

Below, I've captured some of the most common profiles of parents of high school and college students that I've met personally or that I've spoken with in my practice. Do you see yourself in one of them?

Typical Parent Profiles

I Have A Good Rapport With My Teen And A Good Understanding Of What's Next

You're in a great spot with your high schooler. You've made it clear they can come to you and talk about anything. You've been talking about life and career paths after high school, and you're both on the same page. You don't have everything decided, but you both know you can discuss whatever they choose and you're confident that you'll be able to agree on what's best and work together to achieve their goals. Congratulations for having this kind of relationship with your son or daughter. You have a good head start, and the information in this book will help you exponentially in partnering with your high schooler.

I Want My Teen To Have A Good Life – And It's Hard To Step Back

As a parent you want your teen to be successful. You say, *"I want my child to have a good job and live a life they love."* Because of this, you try to steer your high schooler into careers you think will give them a good life—careers you consider to be stable, such as engineering, computer science, accounting, law, medicine, or nursing. But is that the right choice for your son or daughter?

My Child Must Go To College , Whether They're Ready Or Not. They'll Thank Me Someday

You strongly believe that going to college immediately after high school is the only way to have a successful life, and you always assumed your child would go. So, why delay? The sooner they start, the sooner they'll get started with their career. Besides, tuition goes up each year! Some of you parents have saved for college and some of you haven't, but nonetheless it's a given your child will go to college, regardless of the costs. This is so important to you that sometimes you're unable to hear what your son or daughter is saying about their wishes. Your teen may not want to go to college, and with the right discussion and planning, that can be okay.

Here are two situations that I see too frequently in my practice:

Emma's Story

Emma is now 30 years old. Emma was brilliant in high school, but she missed a semester due to illness. As a result, she fell behind. Her parents believed she should attend a specific college, and they did everything to get her accepted, even when she didn't want to go there.

At the time, all she wanted was to attend a two-year community college and take those years to explore her options. Her parents' intent was to help her be qualified for a good job. In the end, she was so miserable she didn't do well in college and graduated after six years with nothing much to show for it. Although quite bright, she felt lost and insecure and had low self-esteem. Despite having a career coach, she hasn't been able to complete the coaching sessions to decide on a career as she no longer has the motivation.

Noah's Story

Noah's story is similar to Emma's. He didn't want to attend college, but his parents insisted he must. He graduated with no career and no interest in what he studied. He is now 35 years old, and his parents are still paying his rent, car, and other expenses while they're both worried that he's not making any progress toward a career.

My Child Must Go To My Alma Mater

It's a family tradition, with a long history of family members attending a particular university. You expect your high schooler to attend the same university, whether they want to or not.

I'm A Hands-Off Parent

Your teen is independent. You'll leave your son or daughter to do whatever they want. Your parents were hands off and you turned out okay, so your teen can do it too.

I Don't Know How To Be Loving And Supportive While Also Giving My Teen Freedom

You love your son or daughter tremendously, and you're so very concerned for their success that you can't see beyond what you consider to be best. You try hard to steer them in that "right" direction and don't trust their judgment. It's difficult for you to face the realization that it's time to set them free. It's not easy for you to understand that as your teen transitions into adulthood and independence, they need you in a different way. They need you to be supportive, to act as a sounding board, and to hear your opinions, but they also need to be the driver of their own journey.

I Want To Help With Everything

You're the classic helicopter parent who tells your high schooler everything that's best for them because you want them to be successful and independent and you know best. You research everything to "help" your teen because they have so much to do and you just want to help.

You don't realize that your son or daughter needs to face issues and do work for themselves. You tell them what needs to be done and how it needs to be done, and then you do it for them anyway.

Summary

Although these profiles aren't indicative of all parents of high school and college students, you'll probably see yourself in one or more of these scenarios. If you do see yourself, keep in mind that this is how your child also sees you. Is there anything you need to reflect on? Anything you need to change to support your teen's career and life?

In Chapter 7, you and your high schooler will be introduced to our T.R.U.S.T.™ system to help you work together and communicate as a team to get on the same page to achieve their career goals. The key is to remember it's **their** career and they'll be living it so it's important they enjoy it.

Chapter 4

Challenges Faced By Parents of High School Students

The role of parents of a high school student can be challenging, and conflicts can be frequent. Your teen is growing up, and your role as a parent can clash with the changes that are occurring in their life as they discover themselves and transition into adulthood. As a result, this can be difficult for both the student and the parent. Below are some of the challenges that parents face.

1. Technology Has Changed The Way Parents And High Schoolers Communicate

In today's world, it seems everyone is using a smart phone from a very young age. There's so much technology around us that we're not talking person-to-person as much as we used to. Even when people are together, they're preoccupied with technology—kids are playing games, teens are Snapchatting, and parents are texting and emailing. This has abbreviated the time available for parents and their high schoolers to communicate. As a result, parents have to make it their business and insist that they and their children make time to talk.

Technology aside, sometimes students don't want to share information or their feelings and thoughts with their parents. Also, parents sometimes don't want to share everything they think. I often observe parents who are hesitant to communicate for fear of appearing too forceful or as if they're trying to push their teen in a certain direction, so they hold back.

2. Differences Of Opinion Between You And Your High Schooler

What you think is best for your high schooler in terms of a career may not always be what they think. In fact, more often than not, this will be the case. Having an open mind is important so you can have honest and productive discussions that put you on the same page.

3. The Perfect Career Of Yesterday No Longer Exists

The world of work has changed dramatically just over the past 10 years, and it continues to do so. What was a perfect career five or 10 years ago may not exist today or could become obsolete tomorrow. According to a recent study by Oxford University, 47 percent of the jobs today won't exist in the next 25 years. So everyone needs to understand that flexibility is required in planning a career for the high schooler. Both parents and student need to exercise that flexibility.

4. Today's Workplace Has Changed

Today, things change so rapidly that it's unrealistic to believe that a person will continue in one career throughout their work life. And even if they do remain in one career, according to the Bureau of Labor Statistics, the average person will change jobs approximately 10 times before they're 40. The days when people started with a career and could actually retire from that same career are just about over. As parents, you will need to keep this in mind as you talk with your teen about their future.

5. Supporting Their High Schooler To Be Their Own Individual

In high school, everything can seem to be life or death, with high schoolers having a great need to fit in and not be left out. As a result, your son or daughter may not reveal what they truly believe or what they want in order to stay in a group. As a parent, your challenge is to help your high schooler stick with their own ideas and interests about what happens after they graduate and not be influenced by what their peers are doing.

6. Co-Parenting Mixed Messages

You're a parent who's doing your best to plan for your teen's future. Your teen lives with you, but whenever he or she sees the other parent, plans change. You feel there's a tug of war, and you can sense the tension in your teen who doesn't want to play favorites or be caught in the middle between you and your ex. You struggle to find the best approach to handle this problem.

Whatever your parental challenge, our T.R.U.S.T.™ system will help you with a framework to discuss these issues with your teen. The system can also help with your ex and your co-parenting challenges, all so you and your high schooler can have a great time planning for the future.

Chapter 5

Technology is Continuously Reshaping the Job Market - Why Do We Need to Plan for Careers?

Many people ask why it's so important to plan for careers when technology makes the world of work so fluid. Even though the workplace is changing, it is critical to understand that career planning is not about a job title but more about recognizing your interests, values, and personality as well as the skills required to do the work that best fits you. A well-planned career emphasizes your best talents, capabilities, and skills that are transferable to other positions and opportunities in another field should your position get eliminated.

Remember, technology also adds jobs to the economy. A recent McKinsey & Company study shows that one-third of the new jobs created in the United States over the past 25 years barely existed or did not exist at all previously. Further, one-third of all new jobs are attributed to information technology. That same study also showed that in France in the previous 15 years the internet had eliminated 500,000 jobs but at the same time technology had created 1.2 million other jobs. By just looking at the numbers, it's safe to conclude that technology will take away some opportunities but will also create many new opportunities.

Planning Is A Lifelong Skill

Even though technology has caused many changes in the workplace, those changes aren't happening overnight. The ability to plan and be forward thinking is a skill that will serve you well throughout your career and lifetime. Sitting back and not planning because technology is "taking over" isn't a good career or life decision.

When Should Students Start Planning Their Careers?

Students should start thinking about what they would like to do for a career in middle school and most definitely by their freshman year in high school.

They should also consider taking some electives or technical classes as soon as they have the opportunity. Electives can help students discover talents and skills they didn't know they had because they'd been too busy trying to keep up with core academic classes. Not everyone is good at math and science, or at English and the social sciences. Electives help students discover other things they may be good at. Students may be surprised to find talents in areas they never knew they had. Sometimes discoveries from these explorations form the basis of the student's eventual career. When students discover an unexpected interest or talent, they can go online and research job possibilities that may be associated with that interest or talent.

Career Planning Is Important Even For Students Who Don't Plan On Going To College

Even students who aren't going to college need to have a plan for what they're going to do as an alternative. Are they going to take a year off and then go to college? Are they going to skip two-year or four-year colleges altogether? Are they going to go to a trade school? Are they planning to work right after high school and if so, doing what? All of these questions need careful consideration—just as much, if not more, than the career planning done by students who are planning to go to college.

Here's Why Career Planning Is Important

Career planning is about helping you find the work activities that are most aligned with who you are. When your skills are in alignment with the work that's right for you, it's much easier to adjust and realign as the environment changes. There will always be foundational expertise and know-how that's required, even in today's technologically advanced workplace.

When you're in a career that's ill-fitted for you, you'll always fight an uphill battle because you're not in sync with who you are and the work you're doing. I can attest to this firsthand from my experience before I became a career professional. I constantly felt insecure because the work I was doing wasn't the right fit for me. After years of working in the wrong career, I hired a career coach and found my true career—my calling—as a career coach. It was my success as a career coach that led me to establish my own company. Now I feel extremely comfortable in the career space, and I'm confident that with just a little adjustment, I'll be ready to take on any challenge.

The point is, even when your actual job title changes, there's still work that needs to be done, whether it's via technology or done manually. Someone still needs to understand what needs to be done. This becomes much easier when you're in the right space in the right industry in the right field of work.

It's about knowing who you are and what you like to do and being able to adapt and adjust as the workplace evolves. The more confident you are and the more you enjoy what you do, the more open you are to be creative, flexible, and receptive to learning new things. The more you enjoy what you do, the more productive you are.

Consequences Of Not Planning

If you don't plan, you can waste a lot of time figuring out what the best occupation is for you, getting you off to a late start as you try to find the right work. You may never experience fulfillment in your work. To avoid this, you'll need to plan—it's one of the most important things you can do in terms of having a good quality of life.

Below are a few examples of what can happen when there's a lack of career planning and a lack of proper communication between parents and their high school students. As you can see, both parents and students lose when this happens, and it's very costly.

Ryan's Story

Ryan, a prospective client, came to me after completing medical school and preparing to start his residency. There was just one small problem—although he cared about people's health and wellness, he didn't want to spend his days working in a doctor's office or a hospital. That simply didn't bring him joy. Instead, he wanted to pursue a career in business. It was a field he'd always been interested in but hadn't gone into because he didn't want to disappoint his family who were all in the medical field.

After career discussions with Ryan we confirmed that business was in fact a better career fit for him. And even though he wasn't going to be a doctor, the good news was he could still take advantage of his knowledge and his love for health and wellness to pursue a business career in the health care field. Depending on his progress, he has the potential for a career that could lead him into management.

Zack's Story

Zack was a smart high school student who was good at assessing situations and drawing conclusions. He was in the debate club, and although an introvert, he enjoyed discussions, was an avid reader, and enjoyed writing. His dad was a lawyer and his mother was a teacher.

Everyone told him he should be a lawyer, and his dad encouraged him toward that goal. Having met Zack, it was easy to see why everyone thought he should be a lawyer. But he also had many other skills and interests, including graphic arts, design, and the outdoors.

When Zack came to us for career exploration, he was stressed and worried about his $250,000 in student loans coming due in a few months.

After working with Zack, we discovered that the best career for him was environmental compliance where he could use his ability to quickly comprehend and interpret laws and present them in a simple manner while working within environmental sustainability. Interestingly, one can be successful in this position with a bachelor's degree! Had Zach worked with a career coach, he could have saved himself a lot of money, frustration, and three years of law school.

Zoe's Story

Zoe, 24 years old, is a psychology major who thought she wanted to dance as a career, although her parents wanted her to be a nurse so she could make a good living with a steady, well-paying job. In college, she soon learned she didn't want to be a professional dancer or a nurse. The schedule was too rigorous for a career in dance and she'd be required to work weekends. And she simply had no real interest in being a nurse.

Even though Zoe was being coached by a professional and had identified some careers that would be ideal for her, she was still scared to discuss her choices with her parents. We can't confirm what Zoe is doing today because she didn't show up for her last appointment and never returned our calls. However, some of the careers that were a fit for her with her bachelor's degree in psychology included being a guidance counselor and human resources specialist.

With proper planning and communication, most, if not all, of the above situations could have been avoided.

I've included some stories here not to scare you, but to provide some real-life examples of what has actually happened to young adults because they made wrong career decisions after high school.

The idea is to help you step back and ponder the decisions you're making, not just for the immediate future, but also for the long-term impact or influence these decisions will have on the rest of your life. Depending on your specific situation, you may have to make hard decisions, even if it means not going to college immediately or never going to college. The idea of not going to college may sound alarming, but it's not. What's alarming is not going to college and sitting around doing nothing at all—now that's alarming.

Chapter 6

Success Defined by Students and Parents

The goal of both parents and their son or daughter in the career planning and decision-making process is success for the student. Success, however, can have different meanings for each person.

When I asked a few parents along with high school students to define what success means to them, I received the responses below. My original intent was to gather definitions from high school students and parents only. However, I realized it would be helpful to share definitions from students in college and young adults who have already graduated so we can see if there are any noticeable differences as they mature. I also found it interesting that some of the male high schoolers weren't able to define success as they hadn't given it much thought as of yet.

Students' Definition Of Success

"Success is when you reflect on the past and can clearly see that you've immensely improved your life since then."

Brooklyn, high school senior who is college-bound

"My definition of success is being able to balance a meaningful, fulfilling career while raising a family."

Lily, high school senior who is college-bound

"I think the definition of success is having achieved your goal and being financially stable. I also think emotionally you'd need to be at peace with the place you're at in life and enjoy it as well."

Adam, high school senior who's not yet sure whether to go to college or take a gap year

"My definition of success is when someone writes a book about me."

Zain, high school junior who is college-bound

"Self-satisfaction and knowing you achieved what you were purposed to achieve."

Kylie, high school senior who is college-bound

"For me success in my life/career would be a well-paying job that's challenging and stimulating but still allows me to have balance."

Sasha, college graduate researching graduate school options

"Being able to contribute to the happiness of those that I care about and to experience life with them. For me, career success is defined by how much I'm moving towards short-term and long-term goals."

Jason, college senior

"I would describe success as financial peace of mind and finding a career you enjoy. The balance of the two can be very different from person to person."

Nathan, recent college graduate

"Having financial stability—not just for day to day but also for paying off loans and saving for a house and retirement. It allows me to access things I love, have a family, and life outside of work. My career is something that feels meaningful and brings me satisfaction."

Sofia, new teacher who recently completed graduate school

Parents' Definition of Success

"Success for my children means a balanced life. Having work that is meaningful to them and provides a good wage so they can live healthy and maintain a relationship with God."

Peter, parent of high school senior who is college-bound

"Success for my daughter would be her becoming independent from me, learning to manage her own life by remembering the things I taught her about life. I encourage her to follow her dream in choosing a career. I believe you're happiest doing something you love and are good at but you always have to have a backup plan."

Savannah, parent of high school senior who is
two-year college-bound

"Success for my child means choosing a career or profession where she can feel fulfilled and still maintain a work-life balance while having strong relationships with family and friends."

Kerry, parent of high school senior who is college-bound

"As a parent, I consider success for my son is when he's working at his best and doing what he enjoys."

Yvonne, single parent of high school graduate who
completed paramedics training

"Success for me as a parent is seeing my child happy and fulfilled. This happiness includes personal, professional, and emotional balance. The bottom line is for my child to go out into the world and be independent and function with confidence."

Logan, parent of two recent college graduates

"I would consider my daughter successful if she loves the work she does, can support herself well, does her job with integrity, and feels she's making a meaningful difference through her career."

Laurel, parent of high school senior who is college-bound

Although this isn't a scientific study, you can see that the definition of success is quite personal, with a wide range of definitions among parents and students. Each group shares a goal for the high schooler or young adult to have a successful life and career after high school. But each also has different opinions and beliefs on what that success should include.

There are a few consistent themes related to how success is defined:

For the high schooler/young adult: Financial stability, work-life balance, and family.

For the parent: Independence, work-life balance, and career fulfillment (i.e., work they love).

As parents and high schooler discuss career and life goals, it's important to ask your son or daughter what success means to them and not take for granted that you know.

Chapter 7

T.R.U.S.T. ™ -Teamwork, Respect, Understanding, Support, Trust

A System For Parents And Students To Partner Together In Career Decision-Making

Getting it right in career decision-making begins with partnership, communication, and trust between parent and high schooler. To work together successfully, candid and open communication is essential, with the understanding that each person has a point of view that should be heard.

I developed a system called **T.R.U.S.T.™**, which stands for **Teamwork, Respect, Understanding, Support, and Trust**, to guide parents and high school students through the communication process so they can have loving, understanding, and fruitful discussions to help in the student's career decisions.

Background To The T.R.U.S.T.™ System

After working with parents and students, it became clear to me that both parents and students had similar challenges. I realized then that I needed to develop a system for effective communication and career decision-making for both parents and students. Using T.R.U.S.T. eliminates the worries and concerns loving parents have about their teen's future. By using this structure, in nearly every case, not only did the parents and students make better choices, but their relationships also improved significantly.

For parents, one of the simplest ways to get you and your teen on the same page begins with loosening up. If you take things overly seriously, everyone gets uptight. Being uptight creates tension, and when there's tension it's hard to relax, which can create an "edge," leading to one or both of you shutting down or to escalated arguments in which the conversation goes nowhere.

Creating an environment of openness, non-judgment, and support is critical to providing an open door so both parents and students are comfortable to talk freely with each other about career and anything else. I often hear from parents and students that they don't know how to talk to one another. One of the key things to remember is that if one person is doing all or most of the talking, that's not communicating— it's delivering a monologue. Communicating is more listening and questioning than talking.

One of the greatest gifts parents can give their child is to be supportive, to dialogue with them about life after high school, and to have an open forum for the exchange of information. Care needs to be taken so that information and ideas aren't delivered in a preaching, condescending manner, but merely as information. Many parents are cautious or reluctant to share but done correctly with the right tone it can be beneficial. Also, if appropriate, parents, show some of your successes and failures; show them that you were a student at one time as well; pause and be that young high school student just for a moment.

As an example, if, after graduating from high school, you as a parent realized it would have been beneficial to have taken a particular high school elective regardless of what you selected to do for a career, that would be good information to share. However, it's not information for you to lay down as law and insist that your teen takes that elective. That wouldn't be communicating effectively as a team; it would be a parent dictating an order and taking away the other team member's (the teen's) opportunity to evaluate and analyze the information to determine if that was the right choice for them.

Please note that by using the **T.R.U.S.T.**™ system, you're not only creating a better planning and decision-making process, you're also helping your teen develop life skills that will be beneficial throughout their career and life.

T.R.U.S.T.™ : Teamwork, Respect, Understanding, Support, Trust

TEAMWORK

Creating an environment of teamwork in which you're both working as equals toward the same goal with the same intentions will remove any perception of conflicting goals from the conversation.

Definition Of Teamwork

To define a team in its simplest form, consider a sports team. Your high schooler is/was probably on a sports team, and you as a parent were probably on a sports team at some point as well. The team is a group of players working together to achieve a common end result: win the game! This "game" is your teen's life. Each individual team member may have his or her own ideas of how the game should be played, but as a team all have to band together with the same goal and function in unity to achieve a common result. They know that's what they have to do to win. The parent/student team is no different.

Working as a team is critical and will drive the entire career planning process, so it's important to get it right. As a parent, you are the team leader as you're more experienced working together as a team, but you're not making one-sided decisions. Everybody's input must be heard, discussed, evaluated, and considered in the final decision-making process.

Characteristics Of A Good Team

- Establish ground rules the team will abide by.
- Identify and focus on the team goal(s).
- Maintain open lines of communication.
- Have respect for each person and his or her ideas.
- Demonstrate respect for each other's opinions.
- Manage conflict.
- Agree to disagree as both members of the team will often not be on the same page.
- Work together cohesively.
- Capitalize on each person's strength and the value he or she brings to the table.
- Know that it's okay to "take a break" and revisit the issue at a later time.

Depending on how communication between parents and your teen is going, it may be a good idea to refer your high schooler to a career coach. Sometimes your son or daughter may not open up as much to you and tell you their true thoughts, such as when you have a particular idea of a direction they should go in and they don't want to tell you otherwise. But a career coach, as a neutral third party, can help students open up and work effectively on ways to handle that communication with you as parents, as a means of finding the best career fit.

Don't hesitate to get help, and do so sooner rather than later, to ensure there's no breakdown in communication that could stall your progress. Even the best teams have challenges and may need support from a coach.

Benefits Of A Team

- Helps emphasize the importance of collaboration and the results that it brings.

- Helps build analytical skills. Often members of a team will have to weigh the pros and cons in decision-making.

- Builds confidence.

- Strengthens communication skills, so team members can voice their thoughts and feelings within the right framework.

- Prepares students for college and the professional world where they'll be working in teams. I know from experience some of these teams can be dysfunctional. Having prior experience in handling difficult situations when partnering with others will put your teen ahead of their college teammates.

- Prepares students for work and makes them more employable regardless of their career choices. One of the first skills people look for when hiring people is teamwork because it's a critical skill in the workplace.

- Forces members to work together toward one goal.

- Capitalizes on each person's strength and what he or she brings to the table.

- Emphasizes importance of trust.

Why Do Companies Use Teams?

- Sharing of different ideas and information is valuable.

- There's power in a highly functional team.

- Brings more resources, skills, and experience to the table.

- Teams have been around since the beginning of time. Even in the Bible, there are references to teams.

RESPECT

We all desire and need respect, and so many people and corporations have respect as one of their core values. But do we always exemplify respect in our actions, words, and attitudes?

Exhibiting respect in family discussions is another great gift a parent can give their high schooler in preparing them for their professional and personal life. Giving respect to others and in turn receiving respect elevates your whole being.

It's important to set up ground rules and agree on terms of how you're going to conduct this "what's next after high school" discussion so that it's handled amicably and respectfully among all parties. Even if it's a situation where you need to disagree, it should be done with respect. Students should be able to appreciate and respect where their parents are coming from and parents should be able to do the same for their teen, understanding that their years of training have paid off by raising an individual worthy of respect.

There are many ways to show respect, and one is simply by listening without interrupting. If someone misunderstands a point or if something causes friction, it's respectful to acknowledge it and apologize if the situation calls for it. This is true for both parents and students.

How To Show Respect

- Be honest and sincere.
- Listen with undivided attention.
- Acknowledge the other person's perspective.
- Don't interrupt with your own ideas when someone is speaking.
- Don't roll your eyes when the other person raises a point you don't agree with.
- Don't yell.

- Don't threaten ("You do what I say or else...")
- Don't slam the door or storm out of the room when there's conflict.

Practicing respect will not only help the discussion process, but it will also enhance the relationship between parents and their high schooler. Showing respect is also about a teen giving parents the respect they've earned by simply being parents and doing their job.

Consequences Of Not Showing Respect

Have you ever worked with a team or been around a group where there's no respect? It inhibits people and eventually they shut down, don't contribute to the conversation, and just tune out. This is certainly not what we're looking for in the team discussion with your high schooler.

UNDERSTANDING

Although parents and students are working toward the same goals, they're coming from different ways of thinking. The student is coming from a place of inexperience in making significant life decisions, whereas the parent is coming from a place of having lived life and knowing the consequences of certain decisions. This can sometimes create conflicts and misunderstanding.

Parents, understand the level of pressure your teen is experiencing to perform in high school and ensure they graduate with top grades. The pressure of determining what they should do after high school is fierce, with everyone asking where they're going to college, even though college isn't the best option for all students.

Some students may be embarrassed or afraid to confess they don't want to go to college. When this happens, it's important for parents to acknowledge their teen's thoughts and feelings and talk things through. Teens, understand that your parents love you but they're coming from a whole different set of life experiences.

Ways To Show Understanding

- Ask for clarification when you're not fully clear on the information.

- Try to put yourself in the other person's shoes. The view is often different from someone else's perspective.

- Repeat, rephrase, and restate information to ensure you're both hearing the same thing.

- Ask questions to get clarification.

- Read verbal or physical cues and body language; this helps in knowing when to say something or when to hold off for another time.

- Create your own handy "do not disturb" signal and use it to show this isn't a good time for discussion and you'll need to talk later.

Why It's Important To Be Understanding

- Understanding helps the relationship between parents and the student—it builds trust.

- This is a tough time for both parents and the student—there are so many big decisions for the student to make. Being understanding will help make things less stressful for all.

- Your high schooler may be anxious and scared of all the decisions and responsibilities that lie ahead. This can be crippling and can result in withdrawal. As a parent, you can help by showing you're there for your son or daughter and available to assist in any way.

- The avoidance your high schooler may be demonstrating by staying in their room is not about you but more about them not knowing how to deal with all the changes that are occurring.

SUPPORT

You can have the best team in the world, but if that team doesn't have support, it's going to lose. Support strengthens. Providing support for your high schooler is valuable not just through this career decision-making process but for their entire life.

Benefits Of Support

- Creates a safe environment for both parties to take chances and explore options.
- Provides strength and confidence – always a good thing!
- Knowing someone "has your back" empowers you to be bold.

How To Show Support

- Have open and candid conversations.
- Be ready and available to participate when asked even though you may not feel like doing so.
- Use positive adjectives to describe each other.
- Do not judge, blame, or assign guilt.
- Be an active participant in the process.

TRUST

How do you feel when someone trusts you? It makes most of us feel great, and it moves our confidence meter up a notch. How about when you make a mistake or a wrong decision and there's someone to give you a second chance, simply because they believe in you and trust you?

As a parent, it's important to demonstrate trust in your teen. Doing this will build their confidence and help them feel empowered as they face life after high school. With trust you must also know that at some point you'll have to let go and be okay with seeing your son or daughter make mistakes. Learning from experience is often the best teacher.

Trust Is One Of The Most Empowering Gifts A Parent Can Give A Teen

- Trust from a parent is a gift that beats any other. It's greater than trips around the world, a new car, or college tuition.
- Knowing their parents trust them is an important confidence booster.
- Knowing their parents trust them will give them permission to take a risk. Realizing big dreams often comes from taking risks.

TYING THE T.R.U.S.T.™ SYSTEM TOGETHER

Now that you have the tools to communicate with your high schooler using **Teamwork, Respect, Understanding, Support, and Trust**, the next step is to put them all together.

As a parent, up until now, you've provided for and made decisions for your high schooler. You've done an amazing job. Your high schooler getting this far is thanks, in large part, to you and your parenting. But now, it's your time to let your teen soar. It's their time for great exploration and discovery, and they may even approach you with a career decision that will make you cringe. But because you have your **T.R.U.S.T.™** system in place, you both can sit back and discuss things and amicably make a decision about which direction to pursue.

Parents, understand that you're not out of the decision-making loop—you're simply using communication to empower both you and your high schooler to talk things through and make decisions in a collaborative manner so that everybody wins.

Chapter 8

Parent and High School Student Team Discussion for Career Planning

Now that parents and students are on the same page on how to communicate effectively, here are some topics and information to have available for your team meetings when discussing the student's career and life after high school.

The College Discussion

Is A College Degree Still Worth It?

Absolutely. There are multiple studies documenting that people with a college degree, in general, earn more than those without a degree over the long term.

Here are some facts and figures to consider:

According to the Federal Reserve Bank of New York, over a 40-year career, a person with a bachelor's degree can expect to earn about $1.2 million more than someone with just a high school diploma. And someone with an associate's degree typically will earn $325,000 more than someone with just a high school education.

However, a college degree without any goal or plan could find you in almost the same position as someone with no college degree. There are thousands, perhaps millions, of individuals who have completed college and who are living no better lives than a high school graduate.

I'm someone who believes going to college is important, and I'm a supporter of education. But what is critical to success is not so much the education but the person behind that education. If you're someone who's a go-getter and you have the drive and you're assertive, you can be successful because you'll capitalize on that education. So, yes, a college degree is still worth it, but you should go to college for the right reasons because if you earn a degree that you're not passionate about, you won't get the benefit.

It is not the advanced degree/education that creates success; it is how the individual takes advantage of the degree.

Success must be driven by commitment, relentlessness, and a burning desire to go the extra mile to get what you want, even when there are obstacles making it difficult. If these drivers aren't in place to make the best of the degree, then it's not worth much.

Does Getting Into College Guarantee Success?

Absolutely not. Getting into college is only the beginning of the future. A degree is not a magic wand. Graduating from college takes commitment, dedication, and hard work. Here are some numbers to consider when thinking about this:

According to the National Center for Education Statistics (NCES):

- Approximately 63 percent of high school students enter college (two-year and four-year) each year.
- 77 percent of college freshmen return for their sophomore year and 23 percent drop out.
- 60 percent of students who enter colleges and universities graduate within six years from four-year bachelor degree programs.
- Only 29 percent graduate within three years from two-year associate degree programs.

A Harvard University study shows one factor in the higher dropout rates is the rising cost of a college education. According to the NCES, the cost of college, adjusted for inflation, has more than doubled in the last three decades. In the United States, 25 percent of borrowers are behind on their loans, and outstanding student loan debt has surpassed an unprecedented $1.44 trillion.

Note: Being aware of this data is important as parents and students discuss whether to attend college or not, the type of college to attend, and the major to pursue. This is where a key portion of discussions should be centered—on the student's willingness to graduate from college with large student loan debt that they will be paying off for the next 20 years. Is it worth foregoing the dream college to attend a less expensive college and graduate without student loan debt or with much less debt?

Factors To Consider When Choosing A College

Now that you have some information that can help you determine whether you'll attend college or not, there are many factors that need to be taken into consideration in choosing a college, most of which center on the cost-versus-benefit analysis, or the return on investment. Is it really worth it to spend $50,000 or more per year for four years for a total of $200,000 plus compounded interest to graduate with a major where you'll still have to learn a skill in order to have a job that pays you a reasonable income?

As you discuss your options and make your plans, also keep in mind that you may decide to earn a master's or other professional degree in the future. This could potentially add another $100,000 or more, plus interest, in student loans.

List Your Criteria For College

Create a list of the criteria you want to use to evaluate and narrow down your college application list. Here are some of the more common criteria:

- Degrees offered
- Majors/minors offered
- College specialization (discipline of study the college is known for)
- Location (rural, suburban, or urban setting and distance from home)
- Size of the student population (from small at 1,000 students to large at 35,000-plus)
- Public vs. private
- Costs (tuition, fees, room and board, travel expenses, etc.)
- Financial assistance packages
- Scholarships, including merit aid
- Campus resources (labs, libraries, computer access, career centers, etc.)
- Graduation rate/time
- Placement success/internship and co-op programs
- Quality/type of companies that recruit on campus
- Accreditation
- Academic enrichment opportunities (study abroad, internships, volunteerism, clubs, etc.)
- Class size
- Faculty access/classes taught by full-time qualified faculty with doctorates
- Quality/reputation/ranking

- Level of pressure to excel
- Safety (campus, community)
- Student body (diversity, gender, etc.)
- Social life (fraternities/sororities, athletics, school spirit, etc.)
- Religious affiliation/independent
- Housing options (residence halls, off-campus apartments, living at home)
- Realistic entry expectations (based on typical student admitted)
- Cost versus return on investment

Note: College without planning creates a false belief that you're on the right path.

Four-Year College vs. Two-Year College

Four-Year Colleges

There was a time when a bachelor's degree was prestigious, but now there are millions of graduates with bachelor's degrees. Some of these graduates are doing great, and others are working low-paying jobs.

A question to consider is how college versus hands-on experience will prepare you for life and for the kind of work you want to do. Everything needs to be looked at in the context of the end goal. Otherwise, everything is simply random and not in sync or in harmony with what's best for the student.

Keeping all the information you have about the pros and cons of a college education—the cost and the benefits—if you're pursuing a four-year college, you may use a worksheet or online tool to evaluate colleges and determine which may be best for you, the student. It will take some time and dedication to gather the information you need, but it's important, and it's better to invest your time now while the cost is nothing than to make the wrong decision and regret it later when the price will be much higher.

Two-Year Colleges

Two-year colleges, community colleges, and some vocational colleges offer two-year associate degree programs at a much lower cost per unit than four-year colleges. After completing all the required classes, individuals attending a two-year college can transfer to a four-year college as a junior to complete an additional two years and graduate with a bachelor's degree.

One of the best things about transferring from a two-year college to a four-year college is that you receive the same bachelor's degree at half the price as the student who paid high tuition for the full four years—you can't beat that! Just make sure the courses you take at the two-year college are transferrable to a four-year school. Check with the four-year school you're interested in before you assume any class you take at a community college will transfer. Not all classes do.

There are other issues to keep in mind if you're transferring from a two-year college to a four-year college. You'll have some adjustments that may be challenging. For example:

- You'll join your graduating class mid-point. Students will have established friendships and relationships with their classmates, and it will take time and work to fit in.

- There are many activities for students in their freshman year that help set the tone for the campus experience which you'll have missed.

- Many universities have programs to help transfer students, but you may need to be more assertive socially to build connections and relationships to enrich your college experience.

- Get involved with campus activities early and take advantage of networking and introductory activities the school offers. Many of these are led by students and can be a great way to become familiar with campus activities and meet new friends.

"Dream" Colleges

You already know your dream college. Perhaps it's an Ivy League school and it's well respected in the field you want to study in college. You believe you'll get a job in your field of study much easier if you graduate from this dream college. Although this school has an expensive price tag, you believe it will be worth it in the long run.

If this is your situation or similar, here are some thoughts for parents and students to consider during their team discussion to determine if it's worth it for you to choose (if you're accepted, since many of these top-ranked colleges accept fewer than one in ten applicants).

Consider These Before Investing High Tuition For Your Dream College

- Are there similar schools or alternatives with a lesser price tag?
- Would your future career be hurt if you attended a less expensive school and excelled?
- Should you save your money for graduate school by attending a less expensive undergraduate program?
- Are there activities you can engage in while on campus to build or strengthen skills so you can be equally competitive in the marketplace after graduation?
- Can you get involved in extracurricular activities relevant to the industry or profession you're interested in?
- Are there opportunities to become a teacher's assistant or undergraduate research assistant for a faculty member in your field of interest?
- Are there opportunities for a campus leadership role in student government?

- Can you complete leadership projects in school that relate to your field of interest?

- Can you complement your education by volunteering—not just doing volunteer work to build service hours but taking leadership roles in volunteering activities?

- Are you able to create your own volunteer project for issues that are of interest to you?

- Can you locate a mentor in your area of interest as soon as possible?

These are a few ways you can leverage a less expensive, less popular school to achieve your college education goal and yet be highly competitive with students from more prestigious schools.

How Will You Pay For College?

There are a small percentage of students whose parents can pay their college costs without any financial burden, but for those who aren't as fortunate, how will you pay for college? Will you be happy graduating from college and being burdened for the next 20 years with a four-figure monthly student loan payment? **Student loans have a high cost and are difficult to eliminate.**

Note: Parents and students, please don't get caught up in the hype of a prestigious college that commands a high price tag if you have to take on large student loans to do so. While it's easy to sign for those loans now, you'll have a rude awakening when you're required to pay them back upon graduation, as well as pay for rent, food, car payments, health insurance, and other basic living expenses.

Where will you find the money to save and enjoy some of what life has to offer?

Even if you graduate as a doctor or lawyer with student loan debt, the loans and payments will be significant. Paying much of your income to loans when you get a job isn't pleasant, especially when you see your friends in other careers making less than you and living with more freedom because they went to a less expensive school.

Wouldn't it be great if you didn't have to pay such huge loan payments regardless of how much money you make? This is something to think about before making the college decision.

Consider this:

- According to the Almanac of Higher Education, of the nearly 20 million Americans who attend college each year, about 12 million, or 60 percent, borrow money to do so. Estimates show that the average four-year graduate accumulates $30,000 in loans, and some leave college with six-figure debt (including their parents' loan).

- The median net worth for a head of household under 40 in the U.S. without outstanding student debt was $64,700, more than seven times the $8,700 net worth in a household with outstanding student loan debt, according to a recent Pew Research Center report. (This is an example of life a few decades out when the student loan is still taking its toll. I don't wish to scare you, but this could be you with $8,700 net worth after all that time and effort.)

Which statistics would you like to be a part of upon graduation from college?

This doesn't mean that you shouldn't go for your dream school. By all means, try for your dream school, if you can comfortably afford it and if you can get accepted. The point is to consider the pros and cons.

Key Tips To Consider When Thinking About College Funding

- **Parents: Don't sell your house or empty your retirement fund to pay tuition.** It's not worth it to let yourself go broke to get your child through college. Will your child be happy that you did that, or will they feel guilty? Avoid liquidating major assets such as your retirement money and your house to put your child through college. These are assets that are almost impossible to acquire a second time and you **cannot and should not** rely on your child to support you in your old age. It will be hard enough for them to support themselves.

- **Student: Apply for financial aid early.** Always apply for financial aid, even if you're not sure you'll qualify. In the U.S., complete your FAFSA (www.FAFSA.gov) form as soon as possible each year so you get your teen in line for financial aid. Financial aid is often distributed on a first-come, first-served basis, and the earliest you can submit your FAFSA form is October 1.

- **Parents: PLUS loan vs. private loan.** Don't just get a PLUS loan. PLUS stands for Parent Loan for Undergraduate Students. There are often other options with private financing that offer viable alternatives and competitive interest rates that you may consider. Also remember that the PLUS loan is **your** responsibility. The student loan is **your teen's** responsibility. As an alternate option, you may want to consider helping your child with payments for the student loan instead of taking out a PLUS loan where you're solely responsible for it.

- **Student: Pursue state and local scholarships.** There are all types of scholarships available for a variety of reasons. It may take some work to write an essay to qualify for some, but that's a small price to pay to get a portion or all of your college education paid for. I've included a link to scholarship sites in the Resources section.

Entrepreneurship

Today, with so many advancements in technology, there are a few students who are starting online businesses as early as middle school. Some students have made hundreds of thousands of dollars before they even graduate from high school, and they have no desire to go to college, at least not right away.

You may be a student who's interested in doing something entrepreneurial, but you may feel pressure to go to college so you can have the security of a formal education. Your parents may not be convinced that the world of work has changed so much that you can actually make a living sitting in your bedroom with your laptop and run a business from there.

Parents, yes, you know being an entrepreneur carries risk as you don't have the backing and support of a large corporation to absorb the risks and failures, and health benefits and retirement plans are all the entrepreneur's responsibilities. However, it's not as risky a career as it used to be in the brick and mortar days when it required a significant amount of capital to get started and keep operating.

Nonetheless, entrepreneurship still takes a lot of hard work to ensure and maintain success. Like any career, anyone thinking of entrepreneurship should do their homework by researching and talking with other entrepreneurs to understand what it takes to be successful. The student has to be resilient as there may be many challenges and possible failures while they're pursuing success. Getting health care is a challenge that needs to be addressed up front. As young adults, with the current regulations in the United States, you may be able to use your parents' insurance until age 26, and as you grow your business you can explore options.

The first thing is for your high schooler to find something they truly love doing and are good at, or find a solution to a problem people have and be able to market that solution in some way. The key is it must be something your high schooler is truly interested in. Entrepreneurship requires dedication and hard work. However, most entrepreneurs will tell you that it's easier to work hard when they're doing something they're passionate about and they're the one reaping the rewards.

Remember some of the great entrepreneurs were very young when they started their businesses and weren't successful immediately. Bill Gates started Microsoft at age 20, Steve Jobs co-founded Apple at 21, and Mark Zuckerberg founded Facebook at 19. Here are some less famous entrepreneurs who also started in their youth:

- Joyce Hsieh, founder of Wild Daisy, who started a $2 million business when she was 13.

- Connor Blakely was 15 when he began a social media agency that grew to serving more than 50 small and medium-sized businesses across the United States.

- Eli Wachs is a social entrepreneur who started High School HeroesX to help high school students meaningfully affect their communities through crowdsourced innovation.

- Anthony "Max" Baron is the founder and CEO of PrepReps, a company he started at the age of 15 to connect social influencers on high school and college campuses with brands looking to grow young loyalty.

- Noa Mintz is the 15-year-old founder of Nannies By Noa, a full-service child care agency, serving families in New York City and the Hamptons.

- Aaron Easaw founded INC.UBATOR, a venture capital firm, when he was a high school sophomore. The firm offers programs and investments designed to grow teen businesses.

Read more about their stories in the Resources section.

Although these high schoolers are successful entrepreneurs, it's not the norm for the teen sitting next to you in class to already have his or her own business. However, I wanted to bring visibility to entrepreneurship and to encourage young adults if an idea comes to you that you feel driven to pursue, consider it. You may be surprised— you may be able to start a business serving your own neighborhood and grow from there. And, social media and the internet can help you get the word out at minimal or no cost.

Should you consider entrepreneurship, you'll need to get involved with entrepreneurship communities online and in person to leverage knowledge.

Taking A Gap Year

Taking a gap year after high school is an option for students who want to take a year off before making any major career decisions. They see this as a way to recharge and explore activities that they didn't have the time or the opportunity to do while in high school. They also see this as the last free time they'll have where they can still consider themselves teenagers before having to face the real world.

The key to having a successful gap year is planning. Otherwise, you could quickly find yourself wasting an entire year with not having learned or accomplished anything.

Before deciding on taking a gap year, assess what you'd like to achieve during the year and how you plan to use your time wisely to do so.

For example, you may decide that taking a gap year can give you some time to breathe and rejuvenate so you can think about the future in a less stressful environment. To make this work, think about what activities you'd like to do in that year. Will you work full-time to experience a particular career field? Will you pursue some other interest such as travel, study, volunteering, or conducting research?

Whatever you decide, create a plan with some target dates of what you'd like to accomplish during the year. It's important to keep focused so the year doesn't turn into two years without any of your goals achieved and a whole slate of missed opportunities.

Another thing to keep in mind when considering whether to take a gap year is how different your life may be from when you were in high school and all of your friends were around.

> **Note:** This is a common complaint heard from students who have taken a year off before firming up their next move. Once their friends head off to college or other career quests and they don't have any fulfilling activities planned, they become disappointed and often regret their decision to take a gap year.

Keep in mind that if you plan to attend college after your gap year, you need to decide if you want to get accepted while in high school and defer attendance for a year or apply for college during your year off. The former may be a safer bet to secure college admittance and not get you too much off track.

If you instead plan to apply to college in your gap year, be sure to choose activities that could boost your chances of getting admitted. Delaying a year so you can work and help with college expenses may be viewed more favorably than taking a year off to travel with no specific purpose. However, if the year of travel is to educate you on other countries because you want to pursue a degree in international studies, then a year of travel could help with college admission, assuming you can demonstrate the connection.

The idea is to plan and focus when taking a gap year.

Jordan's Story

Jordan had applied for college as a senior in high school and deferred her enrollment. She decided she wanted to take a gap year so she could become fluent in Spanish. She loves meeting people and learning their stories. She felt having a good command of a second language, Spanish, would broaden the universe of people she could meet and communicate with.

Initially, she wasn't clear about the career she wanted, but she knew it would be connected with Spanish. Jordan also loves history and thought development work in another country could help her learn the history as well as the language.

She chose Costa Rica and worked with an agency to help her with arrangements to enroll in a language academy. Interestingly, Jordan's roommate was Japanese, and because of this, the only way they could communicate was by speaking in their common language of Spanish. That helped each learn the language faster.

While in Costa Rica, Jordan got an internship doing mission work where she traveled within the country helping people and learning the country's history.

In Jordan's view, her gap year benefited her tremendously in several concrete ways:

- *She felt it was instrumental in helping her be clear on what she wanted to do for a career.*
- *She is now studying Spanish and history with the goal to be a teacher in bilingual education.*
- *She tested out of 12 credits because of her fluency in Spanish, which will allow her to graduate a semester early while saving on college costs.*
- *On campus, she also got a job as a language lab leader teaching an hour-long Spanish conversation class. She also got hired for next school year as a teacher's assistant (TA) for a class for international students.*
- *She was a resource for Spanish translation and interpretation at her summer job at a Fortune 500 company.*

- *She's happy to be able to connect with people in Spanish here in the U.S. as well.*

- *Jordan's advice to students thinking about the gap year:*

- *For the gap year to work out for you, you need to decide if you'll be self-motivated enough to take care of things on your own. You don't have your peers, teachers, and parents to handle problems when they arise. It's on you.*

- *It's a completely different atmosphere than high school. You must stay on top of things.*

- *Try and plan as much as you can, but you **must** try to **trust your own self-motivation** as best you can along the way.*

College Is Not For Me

This can be a dreaded conversation for both parents and students. For many parents, hearing this from your child is heartbreaking. After all, it seems that every "good" job asks for a college education. Many require not only a bachelor's degree but a master's degree as well. And your child doesn't even want to go to college.

But hold on, Mom and Dad. It's not the end of the world. Even though your son or daughter may not want to go to college right now, things can change over time. There are certain jobs requiring a degree they won't qualify for, but if they were interested in those jobs, they'd probably be going to college. Some jobs don't require a college degree, including construction workers, transportation inspectors, power plant operators, and certain types of law enforcement officers, to name a few.

There are millions of people who didn't go to college and are successful and happy. The point is not to imply that everyone who doesn't go to college will be successful, but it's worthwhile to step back a moment, catch your breath, gather your thoughts, and then discuss them with your high schooler.

Consider these facts. As you read earlier, it's taking longer and costing more for students to graduate from college. Only two out of five (40 percent) students who enter a public, four-year college graduate within five years. For two-year colleges, the graduation rate is even lower at 28.9 percent. While it's taking many students more than five years to graduate, other students aren't graduating at all—nearly 30 percent of all students who enter college don't return for their sophomore year. Given this information, high schoolers who know that college isn't for them at the moment can save time, money, and frustrations. Additionally, the option is still there for them to attend college at a later time when it feels right.

Certificate Programs

An educational certificate may be a good option if a student isn't interested in getting a degree or if there's no money to pay for college. Certificates are non-degree awards for completing an educational program of study after high school. Typically, students finish these programs to prepare for a specific occupation in a relatively short period of time, with most certificates taking less than a year to complete and almost all designed to take less than two years.

Certificates are one of the most popular types of postsecondary education awards. According to the most recent data available from the National Center for Education Statistics (NCES), over a one-year period, U.S. schools awarded more than 1 million certificates—more than the number of associate's (942,000), master's (731,000), or doctoral degrees (164,000). About 1.7 million bachelor's degrees were awarded in that same year.

Most certificate programs are designed for people who have at least a high school diploma or general equivalency diploma (GED). People usually earn certificates to help them prepare for a specific occupation rather than to earn a college degree. In some cases, however, a certificate can pave the way to college because certain programs' credits count toward a future degree. And for some people, certificate programs help them prepare for licensure, certification, or other career-related qualifications.

Where people earn certificates varies by field of study. For example, people were more likely to earn certificates in business or information technology at public community colleges, while they were more likely to earn certificates in cosmetology and health care at private, for-profit schools.

The U.S. Bureau of Labor Statistics (BLS) has identified 33 occupations as typically requiring a certificate or other postsecondary non-degree award for people entering those occupations. According to the NCES, the most popular disciplines for certificate programs are health care, personal and culinary services, and mechanic and repair technologies. But people also earned certificates in a wide range of other occupational areas, such as computer and information sciences and security and protective services.

The above information was excerpted from Certificates: A Fast Track to Careers, by the BLS. The full document is included under Resources, if you're interested in more details.

On-The-Job Learning/Apprenticeship

On-The-Job Training: There are many careers which require on-the-job training, such as flight attendants, bank tellers, and emergency dispatchers, that don't require a college degree. These occupations typically have formal on-the-job training programs provided by the employer.

Apprenticeship Training: Some jobs require apprenticeship training. An apprenticeship requires working with an experienced worker to learn the job, along with completing some classroom training. Apprenticeships can range from one to five years, depending on the field of work. Apprentices get paid during training, and the compensation increases once the apprenticeship is completed. Some examples of careers that require apprenticeships are dental laboratory technicians, mechanics, heavy equipment operators, electricians, carpenters, plumbers, welders, and cabinetmakers. Some apprenticeship programs are offered by community colleges in partnership with local work force recruiters and require concurrent school attendance.

A final point to consider about not earning a college degree immediately after high school is that not rushing college may be exactly what the doctor ordered for your high school graduate. Sometimes a small dose of reality is just the push that's needed for students to seriously consider life and goals and to determine if not having a college degree will give them the life they wish to live. Sometimes, taking a step back helps to clarify their goals.

And remember, many high school graduates may decide to go to college later, or they may learn what they really want to do only requires a certificate that they can complete online or at a continuing education college.

The point here is that there are options, and it pays to discuss them.

Joining The Military

As we've seen, for some people, college isn't the best way to learn. This is a personal story of someone I know. Her son, Ian, went to college, and during his first semester he decided college wasn't for him—"it was a waste of time and money." He was miserable and didn't want to return for his sophomore year.

Fortunately, his mother listened to him. He joined the military and served one tour of duty and returned home and joined the police force. Today, he's an officer of the law, loves his job, and everybody is happy.

The military is a viable career option where you not only learn a skill but also get training that's transferable to the civilian world. Like other careers, you must do your research prior to joining. Don't join the military as a last resort because you can't think of anything else to do. This could lead to a negative experience if your heart isn't in it. You should have an interest in where you go, what you do, and how you serve this country, because military service isn't just a job; it's an honorable profession that can be exciting and rewarding if you know what you want to do.

Here are a few questions to ask before you sign up for the military:

What branch of the military are you interested in? Joining the military will provide you with specialized training in any number of fields, depending upon the branch you're considering. Learn as much as you can about each branch of military service and see which one will suit your needs. This way, you can serve your country to the best degree possible.

What skills would you like to develop? The military can provide you with training in a variety of areas such as computers, mechanics, or administrative duties. Give some thought to this so you can get the most out of your service.

Can you handle the commitment? Being in the military takes commitment. Think seriously about the duration of the commitment and the restrictions. Is this something you can handle? Once you enlist, you're under contract with the government, and getting out isn't easy.

Are you fully informed? You must ask all of the right questions before enlisting. Make sure you do the appropriate research and talk with as many people as possible. This way, you won't feel misled or cheated when the reality of your situation becomes evident. Don't listen selectively; actively listen to your recruiter. Make a list of things you need to know about and get informed.

What do you want to do in the future? Some of you will want a military career for life. Others will want to serve and move on to pursue an education or career in the civilian world with the skills you picked up while serving. Keep your future in mind when selecting a job when you enlist to ensure that you'll leave the service with the proper tools for a successful and rewarding future.

Where do you want to live? Look at the locations of the different military bases around the country and around the world. Some of those locations are beautiful and some are not. If that's an important factor to you, keep this in mind as you choose a branch of the military.

The military trains people in 140 occupations. Every recruit signs a legal contract for eight years of duty. Usually, two to six years are spent on active duty; the remaining years are spent in the reserve forces. Many military occupations involve skills that can be useful in civilian jobs. Service members receive basic pay, housing, allowances, and benefits for serving in the military. Tuition assistance at colleges and universities is available.

If interested, please see more details in the Resources section.

Whether To Join The Family Business

The family business is the pride of the family. Often it's been passed down for several generations. Your parents expect you to continue this legacy, but you don't want to—you're interested in biotechnology. You'd like to go to college and eventually work with one of the life sciences companies.

Schedule a convenient time to meet with your family and use the T.R.U.S.T.™ system to guide you as you share your appreciation for the family business and its legacy. Also share your desire to pursue the occupation that interests you. Let your parents know how much joy you get from studying and learning about it and how rewarding it would be for you to establish a career in this field. Let them know you'd support them in finding an alternate solution to your taking over the family business.

Perhaps there's someone else in the family that your mom and dad could train. Perhaps you could still provide support or assistance to the family business in some way while you pursue your new field of study. If there isn't an immediate need to have someone take over the business, perhaps you can work together to create a transition plan so when the time comes, everything is in order and your parents will have had time to work with alternatives. This would enable you to move forward without feeling any guilt.

There is an endless list of topics for discussion in career planning. We have included only a few here while understanding you will also have topics that are personal and specific to your own situations and circumstances.

Chapter 9

Choosing The Right Career

A Successful Career Plan Must Consider Life And Work

In career exploration, young adults need to focus not only on their major and possible career but also on how their future work will integrate with their personal life so they can experience happiness in both. All of this may sound like "adult stuff" that high schoolers shouldn't have to be bothered with at this time, but that's the exact reason why they need to do so. Graduating from high school puts someone on the path to adulthood. Whether a student in high school wants to be bothered with career planning or not, the cost of not doing so will be high later on when they realize they're in a career that's not the right fit.

Below are the key actions a student needs to take while in high school to help determine the career that's the best fit. But it's important to understand that nothing is carved in stone, and as we stated before, students may change their minds multiple times before they graduate—they just need to be able to move forward after the change. Even after they enter the workforce, they will very likely change their minds again. However, students who understand themselves and how to go about exploring careers will be ahead of the game and have life skills they can call upon to pivot and survive changes throughout their careers.

1. Explore And Learn More About Yourself

High schoolers, begin exploring careers in your freshman year. Even at this young age, you can appreciate what it feels like to be prepared for something as opposed to when you're not. For example, have you ever made a mistake and thought homework was due on a certain day and went ahead and completed it, only to learn that it wasn't due until the next day or the next week? How did that feel? After kicking yourself for not getting it right, it felt really awesome. You were all done and you didn't need to worry about it anymore.

Planning early for your career is almost the same thing, except that it's not a one-time thing—it's an ongoing process. This doesn't mean you have to get up every day thinking about what's next in your future career. However, if you wait to think about your career until each time you need a job or if you just take the job that happens to come in front of you, chances are you won't be happy in the work you do.

What Should You Explore?

There are a variety of assessments available to help you learn more about the categories below, including Myers-Briggs Personality Preferences, 16 Personalities, O*net Interest Profiler and the Strong Interest Inventory. Your school's guidance counselor, your public library, the internet, or a private career coach are all resources you can use to help in your exploration and to help you answer questions you may have as you go through the process. You should explore the following areas to help you identify careers or occupations that may be right for you.

Your Likes And Dislikes

Learn about yourself by first thinking about what you like and what you dislike, such as videogames, reading, baking, sports, writing, and technology. Identifying things you like will help you consider these as areas you may wish to be involved in for a career. Similarly, knowing what you don't like will be a good indicator of what you don't want to do in the future.

Identify Your Natural Talents, Values, And Interests

Talents: What are the things you do well naturally without thinking? These are your talents. These may be things that could influence your future career choice, so don't ignore them. It's a good idea to jot them down in a Google Doc, notes on your phone, or in a notebook and research careers that require these skills. Don't get bogged down with this being a master, time-consuming project. Just pay attention, and if you find yourself doing something all the time and if people keep asking you to help them with a particular thing, that may be a sign of a talent that others need and could form the basis for a future career.

Values: In thinking about your values, reflect on what makes you feel good about yourself and what principles are the most important to you. For example, honesty may be especially important to you, and because of this you may want to consider a career where honesty and integrity are highly valued so you'll feel good about yourself each day you go to work.

Skills: The difference between talent and skill is that you're born with your talents and you learn your skills. Because you're young and haven't held a long-term job, you may think you don't have a lot of skills yet, but you do. Are you good at reading, writing, organizing, taking the lead, or math? These are skills used in the workplace. Also, ask your mom, dad, siblings, and friends what they've observed you're good at to help you identify skills you may not have considered. As you experience more of life and the world, you'll learn more skills to add to your professional toolbox. Sometimes talent and skills converge where you can't tell the difference which is which, and in the end, it doesn't matter as each can help you develop your career.

Interests: What are you interested in or naturally curious about? Are you interested in helping people, teaching people to learn new things, science, solving problems, designing, social media, or sports? There are an endless number of things to be interested in that you could consider for a career. To learn more about what careers you can have based on these interests, research them on different websites for free.

Work Environment

The type of work environment that appeals to you is very important since you'll be spending eight to nine hours there every work day. Think about the environment that you'd like to work in. Would you enjoy working in an office in close proximity with other people or would you rather work quietly by yourself? Are you an outdoorsy person who would feel restricted working inside an office? These are all important considerations when thinking about what you'd like to do for the rest of your life or for most of the rest of your life.

2. Research

After you've identified your personality preferences, skills, interests, values, and preferred work environment, it's time to do some research to help you identify careers that are in alignment. You can use online resources and talk with your school guidance counselor, your teachers, your parents, friends, and family to help you in your selection process. One of the most widely used online career tools in the United States is www.onetonline.org.

Informational Interviews And Job Shadowing

Once you've conducted research on identifying occupations and careers that appeal to you, you then need to conduct informational interviews. That's when you'll talk directly with people who are doing this kind of work to get first-hand information on the job—what it entails on a daily basis, and the challenges and rewards. To get the most value from your meeting, your questions should focus on getting answers for information that is not already available on the internet and be specific to what's involved in doing the job. Some examples of the types of questions include:

- What does it take to be successful in this career?
- What are some of the things I can do in college to prepare me to get a job in this field upon graduation?
- Does this career typically require extended hours beyond a 40-hour work week to be successful?
- Does this career typically require a high percentage of travel (such as consulting)?

Also explore the opportunity to job shadow. Some schools have relationships with businesses and help students connect with employers who are willing to have students job shadow so they can learn more about the careers that interest them.

3. Getting Work Experience

Internships

Learning more about what you'd like to do by getting some hands-on experience is ideal. It may take some effort to get internships while in high school. However, there are still companies that have relationships with schools that will allow high school students to work during the summer or year-round. Parents, other relatives, and their friends may be able to help you secure internships. There are also a number of internship opportunities posted on the internet.

Part-time Jobs

Some students take on part-time jobs while in high school, and you may want to consider getting one as well. Many of these jobs aren't specifically in their interest area, but they provide students a chance to develop a work ethic and discipline. Part-time jobs give students an understanding of the responsibility of having a job and the need to work within the specific job requirements under the direction of a supervisor. Of course, it's even better if students can find a job in some of their areas of interest to test them out.

Volunteering

Volunteering is a great way to get experience in your area of interest. Although you don't get paid, you have an opportunity to learn about the work and perform in a professional environment with specific responsibilities while learning about a particular business or nonprofit organization.

Whether it's an internship, part-time job, or volunteering, each of these opportunities helps you learn about a business and build accomplishments you can use to create a résumé. But there's also an important side benefit—these opportunities allow you to develop relationships with employers and other supervisors; you'll be able to use them as references for jobs you apply to in the future.

Putting The Career Plan Together

Now that you've done your research and you understand more about yourself and about some possible careers of interest, create a spreadsheet or a table listing the job category, possible job titles, the education required, and any additional information you've learned. Work through this list with your parents and prioritize what's important to you to help you determine which of the careers you've researched and explored best fits you.

If your career planning and exploration determines that college is right for you and you're ready, that's great. You can begin or continue with your college research to determine which colleges are best for you. You now have all the tools to make your decision.

If you decided that college is right for you but you need to take a gap year, put a plan together with specific things that you'll be doing and show how a gap year could help you achieve your future goals.

If you decide that college is not for you at this time, put your plan together on what you'll be doing for a career, such as getting an apprenticeship, joining the military, obtaining a certificate, or working full-time in a certain field.

Here's a quick layout of a sample plan:

Name:

Date:

Career path/occupation:

Education/training level required for entry into this career path:

Colleges I'm interested in that offer this major:

Skills I currently have but need to build on for this career:

Skills I don't have but will need to develop for this career:

Key persons to reach out to /network with:

Chapter 10

A Story of Determination to Succeed At All Costs

To this point, we've focused primarily on parents and students working together for career planning.

But what if the student's parents aren't able to help with career planning? What if the parents speak a different language and no one in the family has ever been to college and they just don't understand the whole career planning process? What if the parent is a single parent with two jobs and simply doesn't have time to help their high schooler?

This story illustrates how one high school student, Daniela, overcame many obstacles to achieve her dream career and is now working doing what she loves.

While I was writing this book, I visited the library many times so I could have quiet time to write. On a number of occasions, I noticed a young lady studying. Needing real-life information for the book, I decided to ask her what she was working on since I'd seen her so many times. I told her about my book, and she agreed to talk with me but asked to schedule a time because she was preparing for a test to obtain her nurse's license.

I asked her how she'd decided she wanted to be a nurse, and she told me she didn't initially know—she just knew she wanted to be in the medical field. Her mother had been sick all of her life and was in and out of hospitals. Seeing how the nurses and physicians cared for her mom and feeling so thankful for their care, Daniela decided she wanted to give back something to the medical profession. She'd felt this way since she was 11 years old.

Daniela's native language is Spanish. When she moved to the United States at age eight, she spoke no English, and when she went to high school there was only one person speaking Spanish in her class. By necessity, she quickly became fluent in English as there were no special classes for her.

Through her senior project in high school, she had the opportunity to work at a hospital. The experience solidified her dream of becoming a registered nurse.

To have her senior project approved, Daniela made numerous phone calls and wrote many emails before a hospital agreed to allow her to shadow because of privacy regulations related to patient confidentiality. However, she persisted and got an opportunity to learn firsthand what it was like to be a nurse. She loved it! She also proved to be valuable as she was able to help with Spanish translation.

Daniela's senior project required 15 hours of job shadowing at the hospital. She enjoyed it so much she asked for approval for an additional 15 hours. Her project also required research. Daniela stayed focused by researching everything she could about being a Registered Nurse. Some of the items she researched included:

- What does it take to be a Registered Nurse (RN)?
- What classes do you need to be an RN?
- Do you need an associate's degree to be an RN?
- Do you need a bachelor's degree to be an RN?
- Do you need a master's degree to be an RN?
- What is the average starting salary for an RN?

Daniela said many people didn't believe in her—they said her English wasn't good enough and she should just accept that she wouldn't get a job at the level of a nurse. (By the way, she spoke excellent English.) But when people told her she wouldn't make it, she focused harder. She didn't allow their negativity or doubt to deter or distract her. In fact, she used it as a propeller to launch herself forward. She knew what she wanted to be and she wouldn't be discouraged or put off track.

Supporting Her Family While Attending High School

Daniela held two jobs while attending high school. Her supervisors were supportive and they worked with her schedule so she could attend classes in the morning to mid-afternoon then go to work. When she got paid, her money went to support her family. She received take-home pay of $422 every other week. Of that amount, $400 went toward rent for the family and the balance of $22 was hers to keep.

Daniela didn't have a phone until her senior year in high school when she could pay the bill from her part-time job.

She went through all of high school **without a computer!** In her senior year when she got a smart phone, she was able to type her documents on the computer at the library and save them by sending an email to herself with the documents as attachments.

She had a difficult time with math, and there was no one at home to help her and her job didn't allow her much time to study. However, she told herself failure wasn't an option, so she made the time between work and classes to study and practice her math using the computer at the library.

Daniela spent almost all of her time outside of work and school at the public library in her area. "This is where I grew up," she told me. Occasionally, one of the librarians would help her, although they couldn't spend much time with her since they had to work. But Daniela was determined and persevered.

First In Family To Graduate From College

Daniela successfully graduated from high school and went directly to college to study nursing. She continued her two jobs while in college and earned an "A" average. While in college, she got married and became pregnant. In the maternity ward, her nurse cared for her in the gentlest manner, which further validated that she was on the right career path.

Daniela was so motivated to stay on track to be a nurse that three days after the birth of her son, she went back to college to continue her nursing studies. She said everyone was expecting her to drop out because of the baby but she knew she wouldn't. And, how do you like this? She got an A in the class.

Daniela was the first in her family to graduate from college. She is now happily working a single job as a nurse.

Her husband is excellent support. He works full time and coordinates his time with Daniela.

Daniela is now a nurse with an associate's degree and will be pursuing her bachelor's degree in nursing. She's happy with her career, and she made it work against all the odds.

Note: Although Daniela knew she wanted to be in health care because of the way the medical profession cared for her mom, she wasn't sure what career to pursue. She remained focused; she did all the research; and she did the job shadowing. These actions helped narrow down and validate nursing as her career choice.

Chapter 11

12 Tips For Successful Career Planning

As you experience life, you'll understand that career planning is an ongoing process and it will build chronologically upon your experience, education, and training, evolving over time. As you enter the first phase of planning your future, these are the top 12 tips for successful career planning.

1. Believe In Yourself

You're the foundation for whatever your future holds. You must believe in yourself and trust you can do whatever you set your mind to do. There will be times when you'll have doubts and will become unsure, mostly because you believe you have to be perfect at something before you qualify for it. Well, you know that's wrong from the start as no one is perfect. "Perfect," in fact, is our biggest enemy as it follows us around and stops us from taking risks and going for our big goals. When you believe in yourself, you throw "perfect" out the window and just "go for it"!

2. Be Honest And Open With Your Parents

Speak regularly with your parents and let them know your true feelings. Use them as your support system and know that you don't have to make all the decisions on your own. Whether you agree with your parents or not, be respectful. This doesn't mean that you should lose your voice and your individuality in exchange for theirs. What it does mean is that you should speak to them using the right language, by acknowledging their points and by expressing your points respectfully.

3. Set A Career Goal And Write It Down

Students, because your decisions today will in one way or another impact your life forever whether you're thinking long term or not, every decision needs to have some thought behind it.

Starting with a primary goal will help you focus for the long term. Write your goal down. Seeing it in writing makes it more real than keeping it in your head. It also helps you keep your plans in alignment with your goal. While aiming toward that goal, it's important to remember to be true to yourself and what motivates you.

The future you're looking into is changing so rapidly that it's critical to be flexible and understand that a changing work environment is the constant in which your generation and future generations will work.

4. Don't Limit Yourself To One Career Idea

Options are great; they give you an opportunity to try other things that you probably wouldn't have considered otherwise. While you're in high school, it's safe to think about other skills or interests. Google is your friend. Just Google "Careers in [whatever field you're interested in]" and see what turns up. From there, you can research further if it piques your interest. The point is not to box yourself in. Options help you eliminate careers that aren't of interest; include careers you'd never thought of before; and provide an opportunity to confirm if the career you're considering is the right fit.

5. Think About The Life You Want To Live As An Adult

Even though you're just entering adulthood, you have many years ahead of you. You may be tempted to think, "Why do I have to be concerned about my whole life now? I'm just graduating from high school."

You're right. You are just graduating from high school, but the more you can think ahead, the better your decisions will be tomorrow.

This will help you save time in the future, and it will also help save you money as you'll spend less time and money re-adjusting or modifying your career as your life evolves.

6. Understand That The Road To Success Is Not A Straight Path

I recommend you take all the goal-setting and planning you're doing in stride. Success doesn't come from one perfect move. Throughout your life (and not just with your career), you'll find that all great plans will have kinks in the road, and only those who are able to adjust will ultimately be successful. Know that you'll often have to modify your plans to respond to the immediate unexpected, but your ability to respond to changes will be the catalyst to propel you forward.

7. Research And Talk With People Working In Your Career Of Interest

In today's world, everything seems to be done through social media. And certainly social media is great for making an initial contact with someone, but you need to take it offline after that. Good, old fashioned face-to-face contact is the best way to communicate. Talk with people in your age group; students in their freshman or sophomore years in college; students graduating from college; recent graduates; and adults in your parents' age group. This will give you a broad range of perspectives and help you think about things from not just yours or your parents' points of view.

8. Plan And Think Big Picture

Planning doesn't need to be tedious. Although it's important, it shouldn't be too intense or pressure-filled for you as a high schooler. You can start planning by simply thinking about what subjects you enjoy and writing them down. Then, as you begin to explore various career options through your research, use the T.R.U.S.T. system on a regular basis to discuss your ideas with your parents. Keep in mind, as a high schooler or new high school graduate, you have only just begun to look into the future of what life will be like with the lens of an adult. Because of this, your world is still narrow. Don't let this limit yourself based on where you are today. Think big picture. Thinking big picture allows you to think beyond the present and look into the future for the potential of what's possible. If you do this, you'll have a solid plan for your future.

9. Find a Mentor In Your Career Or Industry

Finding a mentor in your career field will be beneficial in helping you understand in greater detail what it takes to be successful in that career. A mentor is a more experienced person who will be able to help guide and direct you as you pursue your career. As you gain experience, you may change mentors or get additional mentors depending on your need. An effective mentor understands that his or her role is to be dependable, engaged, authentic, and tuned into your needs as the mentee. Your parents or teachers may be able to introduce you to people who are good candidates as mentors.

10. Use Social Media Wisely

Social media has a lot of advantages and perhaps an equal number of disadvantages. One of the first things people do when they hear your name is to Google you, so it's important to be careful of what you post on social media. The rule of thumb is if you wouldn't want your grandmother to see it, then it shouldn't be on social media.

Adjust your privacy settings so that you have to approve any pictures or comments friends tag you in. This is important because you don't want inappropriate information about you on social media as it can negatively affect your reputation with prospective employers and other persons you'd like to connect with in a professional manner. Also, make sure you have the highest level of privacy on your accounts.

Keep your social media sites respectful. Be mindful of the pictures you post and the comments you make. Know that the people who are conducting online searches for you may be colleges, scholarship providers, future employers, and other professionals. Your social media presence will give them an idea of who you are, so think of the type of person you are when no one is watching. You can create a good impression by posting responsibly.

11. Practice Good Money Management From Your First Paycheck

Whatever you decide for your career, unless you become the founder of some major, world-changing technology, the money you make will have a much shorter lifespan than you ever imagined. That's why it's so important to create a budget before you get your first paycheck and stick with that budget so you always live within your means.

Please see the article on investment in the Resources section, titled "College Grads: Hold Off on Living Large." It's a bit dated, but the concept still holds true today. When I ran a leadership development program at a Fortune 500 company, this was one of the key handouts that I gave every participant, regardless of their background.

12. Have Fun!

Even though you're looking into the future, you're still young, and this is the time for you to enjoy your youth. Don't be stressed! It's exciting to think ahead to when you're an adult and are pursuing a career you love. The ideas we're sharing here are simply for you to start thinking about that new life you'll be leading and make sure you're prepared to get there.

Chapter 12

Significance of Setting Goals

"The most important thing about goals is having one."

Geoffrey F. Abert, Author

Setting goals is an important part of life. Goals help you remain focused on what you want to achieve and the steps you need to take to achieve them. As high schoolers grow more independent, it becomes more important for them to set and work toward goals to ensure their future success. Their goals may include personal accomplishments, careers, academics, relationships, and post high school plans. As a parent, the more you help and support your high schooler to achieve these goals, the greater the chance that will happen.

Parents, it's a good idea to talk with your high schooler about your own goals and share your experiences related to the joys and challenges in attaining them. Your son or daughter can learn from hearing about your goals when you were younger, as well as your successes and failures related to them. Sharing your current goals will also help your teen understand that setting various goals, whether personal or professional, is a life-long process.

Having sharp, clearly defined goals that students can measure will allow them to take pride when they accomplish them. They can see clear, forward progress in what otherwise might have seemed a long, drawn out process.

By setting goals students can:

- Improve their academic performance
- Increase their motivation to achieve

- Boost their self-confidence
- Increase pride and satisfaction in their performance

The basics of goal setting includes: expressing goals positively; establishing priorities; writing goals down so you can be visually reminded of them; keeping goals attainable; setting timelines for achieving goals; setting goals that allow you to have control over the results; and setting goals that are specific and measurable.

By setting goals and measuring their achievements, students are able to see what they have done and what they're capable of. Seeing their results gives them the confidence and assurance they need to believe they can achieve even higher goals.

Chapter 13

The 21st Century Workplace

What Is The 21st Century Workplace?

The workplace of the 21st century is very fluid. It's so much more flat than before, with less hierarchy, and it moves very fast. Since it moves so quickly, you have to be nimble when it comes to your career. You can't be too set on what you think you're going to be doing forever because things keep changing and you have to be open to it. Even as a high school student, know that whatever you start off doing for a college major or when you enter the workforce will most likely not be what you wind up doing. However, the skills and the expertise that you develop will afford you the ability to adapt and adjust as the workplace demands.

The key thing to remember is that in the workplace of the 21st century you have to be flexible and keep an open mind. No skill is ever wasted, but just be ready to transform those skills and launch them into other areas of work.

How Will The Demands Of The 21st Century Workplace Impact The Career A Student Selects Now?

The careers you select today are the careers that are here now. As time evolves, occupations will change, but we don't know how yet. However, having the mindset that change is inevitable and that's not a bad thing is preparation in itself.

As an example, think about the field of medicine. You might believe it's a fairly stable field where much doesn't change but then consider the massive number of technological advances that have taken place in the past fifty years, from less-invasive surgical techniques to digital imaging used in diagnostics. Years ago, learning you had cancer was often tantamount to a death sentence. Not so today, with many types of cancer having tremendously high survival rates, thanks to innovations in chemotherapy, radiation, and other treatments. So doctors, while still delivering their core service of caring for and healing sick people, are constantly having to adopt and embrace changes in medicine.

But as they do so, doctors need different skills, including technological skills in almost every aspect of their work. In the past, for example, medical records had to be mailed or hand delivered. Today, electronic records can be accessed immediately. Doctors who graduated from medical school decades ago probably couldn't anticipate the huge number of changes technology has brought to their practices. The same is likely true for you, no matter what occupation you go into. Even if you stay in the same field for all of your work life, the way you execute your job is destined to change as technology advances.

What Happens If Jobs Get Eliminated?

So, yes, with ever-changing technology, some jobs will be eliminated while others will be created. Some people have a fear of robotics taking over their jobs. A point to remember is that there needs to be someone operating the robotics. So a high schooler today should include coding as one of their classes even if they're not thinking of becoming a software developer. Just having knowledge of basic computer programming will be an asset in tomorrow's workplace.

Being agile and open minded will help you land your next opportunity if your job becomes obsolete. You need to be ready to regenerate and adapt to the work environment because that's the reality of today's work environment, and it will become an even greater reality in the future.

Q: Should I Be Thinking About More Than One Career?

You should always think about what you're good at and what excites you. Your career will evolve, but you don't need to be trained in multiple careers at the same time. However, you should consider how to broaden your knowledge to advance to the next level. It's not about limiting yourself to one career but rather about building on your expertise so that it makes you more valuable and more marketable not only to the company you're working for at the time but to others in the future because you have multiple skills. Think of multiple skills within the career you do so you're easily adaptable. You can then quickly adjust to whatever opportunity may come your way in this changing workplace.

Q: What Are Some Of The Skills Needed In The 21st Century Workplace?

The needs of the workforce in the 21st century have been the subject of numerous studies. Naturally, technology is a given, and as a high schooler you are a technology native so that's not a skill to adopt but one that's already natural to you.

In a study by Hanover Research, the key skills needed to succeed in the 21st century workplace are as follows:

- Collaboration and teamwork
- Innovation
- Creativity and imagination
- Critical thinking
- Problem solving
- Flexibility and adaptability
- Global and cultural awareness
- Information literacy
- Leadership

- Civic literacy and citizenship
- Oral and written communication skills
- Social responsibility and ethics
- Technology literacy
- Initiative

Q: What Is Your Key Takeaway For High Schoolers?

The career choices you make today are going to be with you forever. If you just spent four years of your life studying something you don't want to do, it may seem you've wasted four years of your life, but education is never wasted. It's not ideal, and you've spent money that would have been better served on something you really wanted to do. However, the ability to bounce back and leverage that knowledge into something else can help you move forward instead of looking backward.

That said, your progress would have been much further along if you had done the planning before you went to college. So putting the time into planning and having an understanding of what your life will be like after high school and/or college is extremely important. That determines your future, and that's where it starts.

In closing, the college degree is still valued in the 21st century workplace. People who are successful will be the ones who are flexible, creative, and innovative and who are adaptable to whatever the workplace demands. You are one of those persons!

Chapter 14

Bonus - Career Tips for Moms Returning to Work

This chapter is for moms who exited the workplace to stay at home and take care of their children until they graduated from high school. Now that they've graduated, you'd like to return to work. But how do you go about it?

You may have been in the workforce before or you may be planning to work outside the home for the first time. So why do you want to get into the workplace—what do you hope to get out of it? That's the first thing for you to consider.

You may want to feel a sense of purpose, with money being a secondary consideration. Or you may want to return to the work you were doing before you quit to stay home with your child. Or you may need to earn a second income, perhaps because of the steep cost of college for your high school graduate.

Whatever your reason for wanting to work at this time, one of the key things to understand is that the world of work is a lot different from how it was five years ago, and even more different from how it was 18 years ago. Many positions no longer exist, the hiring process has changed, and more technical skills are required for most positions.

Getting Started

To get started, begin by letting people you interact with know that you're thinking of getting into the workforce. Let them know what your interests are. Consider joining a mom's meet-up networking group. This is helpful because it places you with mothers who may have similar interests or who may be interested in going to work at a future date. You can trade information about your background and experiences to learn about different careers.

Some of you may not have worked outside the home before and may think you don't have any marketable skills. However, this is simply not so. As a parent, you have organizational, leadership, time management, communication, leadership, and other skills you've used over the years to stay on top of your household and keep it running smoothly.

Many of you have held leadership roles in your child's Parent Teacher Association (PTA) or similar organizations. You may have planned events, led committees, managed projects, written newsletters, written blogs, or chaperoned groups of children on field trips.

Some of you may have chosen volunteer work strategically in order to hone your skills. Or you may have invested heavily in different types of training. All of these will be helpful for you to draw upon when evaluating your skills and readiness for the workforce.

Depending on the path you decide you'd like to follow, below are some actions you'll need to take to get ready for this next chapter of your life:

Preparing For The Job Search

- Enhance your technology skills so you can fit right in with the rest of the workforce, e.g., Microsoft Office including Word, Excel, PowerPoint, and Outlook.

- Demonstrate your knowledge of social media. Many stay-at-home mothers are experts with Facebook and other social media outlets and could highlight this as one of their strengths.

- Become an expert in whatever field you're interested in. Research the topic on Google.

- Upgrade your credentials. Based on your interest, a certificate program at a local community college or an adult extension college may be a great option.

- Create a whitepaper on your area of interest and try to get it published professionally, or simply start a blog online.

- Take advantage of free resources online to help you craft an updated résumé and build your interview skills.

- Highlight the value you'll bring to the company now, rather than your time away from paid work.

- If you have prior experience, showcase your past work successes in specific terms, as if they happened yesterday.

- If you don't have prior experience, showcase all the activities you've led or participated in as accomplishments, emphasizing the skills you've applied to achieve success.

- Create a LinkedIn profile and connect with people from your high school, university, and local community, as well as any professionals you know. This will help you build a wide network and give you visibility to employers.

- If asked about the gap in your career, explain your career break briefly and in positive terms, then move on. For example, you may relay that during your time away from the traditional workplace you completed professional development in a number of areas and helped ABC charitable organization with its XYZ project.

- Take advantage of National Career Development Association (NCDA) and CareerOneStop resources.

- If you're having challenges doing it on your own, retain the help of a career coach to help you put things together professionally and get you prepared for the workplace.

Consider Starting Your Own Business

As a stay-at-home parent, you've developed skills in parenting that others would like to learn. Perhaps you have special expertise in handling difficult situations with a child with special needs and you've had to do endless research and navigate bureaucracy to find the right help for your child. These are skills you can share with others, whether in blog or magazine articles or in a book. You could also coach others on how to get the help and resources they need for their child. The beauty of this is that you can do this kind of job from home and set your own hours while serving a worthy cause.

You may also consider freelance work using the skills and expertise you amassed before you became a stay-at-home mom. Or you may be able to capitalize on skills you developed while parenting. For example, you may have been the photographer at school events and managed your PTA's social media account. If you find that people ask you to help them with a skill you have, you can consider charging for your services and launching a freelance career.

These are just some ideas for you to think about as you consider getting back into the workplace. Not everyone will have the same goals for the work they'd like to do. The most important consideration is thinking about what you'd like to do and how your skills and talents can help you achieve your goals.

There's an opportunity waiting for you!

Resources

These are some of the resources available for students and parents that I find the most helpful.

Guide to Life after High School - Mapping Your Future

This site provides information about careers, academic preparation for college, how to pay for college, and managing your financial life after high school graduation.

www. mappingyourfuture.org/guidetolife/

Bureau of Labor Statistics

The Bureau of Labor Statistics (BLS) is a unit of the U.S. Department of Labor. It is the principal fact-finding agency for the U.S. government in the broad field of labor economics and statistics and serves as a principal agency of the U.S. Federal Statistical System.

www.bls.gov/careeroutlook/

NCDA – National Career Development Association

The National Career Development Association (NCDA) serves professionals in the career development field. I recommend starting at this site because there are a variety of categorized resources available under their Resources link.

www.ncda.org/aws/NCDA/pt/sp/resources

Certificates: A Fast Track to Careers

This site lists a number of occupations that require only a certificate that can be earned from a two-year college or trade school, or online.

www.bls.gov/careeroutlook/2012/winter/art01.pdf

O*NET OnLine

O*NET OnLine has detailed descriptions of the world of work for use by job seekers, workforce development and human resources professionals, students, researchers, and more.

www.onetonline.org/

Occupational Outlook Handbook (OOH)

The OOH can help you find career information on duties, education and training, pay, and outlook for hundreds of occupations.

www.bls.gov/ooh/

CareerOneStop

CareerOneStop is a comprehensive website with resources and tools for any stage of the career development process. The website includes tools for exploration and self-assessment; educational options and information; occupational information; and salary and economic trend data.

www.careeronestop.org/

California Career Zone

The California CareerZone is a web-based career exploration system available to all Californians free of charge. Other states may offer similar resources.

www.cacareerzone.org/

Choosing the Right College

The College Board is a mission-driven, not-for-profit organization that connects students to college success and opportunity. It administers the SAT and AP exams, and has useful information on paying for college and finding scholarships.

bigfuture.collegeboard.org/

College Confidential is the internet's largest resource on choosing colleges, getting into college, and paying for college. It offers a wealth of information for both parents and students, including a very active message board on all topics related to college.

www.collegeconfidential.com/

Café College is another site to help you choose the right college.

www.cafecollege.org/seniors/discover-your-options/find-a-college-that-fits

Scholarships Sites with Reviews

www.reviews.com/best-scholarship-search-platforms/

Creating a LinkedIn Profile

"18 Tips to Create Your Perfect LinkedIn Profile"

www.entrepreneur.com/article/271919

High School Entrepreneurs

www.startupgrind.com/blog/5-high-school-entrepreneurs-to-watch-in-2016/

Joining the Military

"Things to Consider Before Joining the U.S. Military"

www.thebalance.com/things-to-consider-before-joining-the-us-military-3353995

Financial Advice for When You Start Working

"College Grads: Hold off on Living Large"

daradollarsmart.com/LATimes6-08-08.pdf

About The Author

Juliet Murphy, MBA is the President of a full-service career management company, Juliet Murphy Career Development (JMCD), delivering career solutions to young adults, executives and corporations. Specialties include career empowerment coaching and millennial career development, with Murphy having a strong background in working with new college graduates. Before starting her private practice, she led an award-winning leadership development program for new college graduates for a Fortune 500 company.

Murphy's passion for helping young adults stems from her growing frustration from seeing many students graduate college with no clue as to what they'd be doing for a career. This led Murphy to design a system to help both parents and students in the career decision process.

Murphy earned an MBA from the University of Southern California (USC) Marshall School of Business and has a Master's in Career Development from John F. Kennedy University. She is the co-chair of the USC Marshall Undergraduate Advisory Board, where she helps the school's educators plan curriculum for their undergraduate business programs. Her business website can be found at www.julietmurphy.com.

Murphy and her husband, Brian are the parents of two recent college graduates.

Acknowledgements

Thank you to all my family and friends who encouraged me and were so very patient when I was unavailable for so many events and activities while I wrote this book.

Alanna and Dylan: The best kids Brian and I could ever have hoped for.

Opal, JP, Simone, and Xavier: I'm blessed to have you as my family and cheerleaders.

Connie, my mother-in-law: For your support and words of encouragement.

My Jamaican "sisters" Ann and Opal Dawn: Thank you for your loyal support over the years.

Beth and Terri, my dear friends: Thank you for always checking on me and helping me to keep the balance even though that was not always possible.

My "Mixed Greens" family: Barb, Gloria, Lauren, Jill, and Yvonne, thanks for the advice and fun during our girls' trips which I always made time for.

Pat, my assistant: For keeping the office in check.

The many people who contributed to the book in different ways, including Dr. Wall, Pam, Vickie, Mike, Gabby, Lauren, Morgan, Susannah, and a few whose names I did not capture.

My clients, who are my inspiration for this book.

My amazing editor, Cindy: I could not have asked for anything more in an editor. Thank you, Cindy!

Mike Koenigs, Ed Rush, Susan Ordona and Alicia Dunams: Without your professional help, this book would still be in progress.

Lisa Sasevich: For introducing me to Mike and her gift to make his training a reality for me.

Darnyelle Jervey: My business coach.

Work with Juliet

Start Your High Schooler Off With The Right Choice for Their Life and Future Career

Contact Juliet Murphy for a Strategy Session

Juliet Murphy's Parent & Teen coaching program is changing the way parents and their high school students partner together to make the best career choices. If you want your high schooler to make the right choices so they will love the work they do and live the life they desire, contact:

Juliet Murphy

JULIET MURPHY CAREER DEVELOPMENT

info@julietmurphy.com

(949) 385-2411

www.julietmurphy.com